Family in America

Family in America

Advisory Editors: David J. Rothman

Professor of History,
Columbia University

Sheila M. Rothman

THE BANKRUPTCY
OF MARRIAGE

V. F. CALVERTON

ARNO PRESS & THE NEW YORK TIMES
New York   1972

Reprint Edition 1972 by Arno Press Inc.

LC#   76-169403
ISBN 0-405-03852-6

Family in America
ISBN for complete set: 0-405-03840-2
See last pages of this volume for titles.

Manufactured in the United States of America

THE BANKRUPTCY
OF MARRIAGE

THE BANKRUPTCY
OF MARRIAGE

V. F. CALVERTON

NEW YORK

THE MACAULAY COMPANY

MCMXXVIII

PRINTED IN THE UNITED STATES OF AMERICA

To
SAMUEL SCHMALHAUSEN
one of those few rare souls
who has dedicated his intelligence to the task
of making life a thing of beauty and
not a thing of escape

PREFACE

THAT the present chaos in modern morals is a theme which demands wide and intelligent consideration can scarcely be denied by radical or reactionary. Many radicals, it is true, may regard the change with a regret and caution characteristic of conservatives, and there also will be reactionaries who may greet the change with the enthusiasm of radicals. These divergencies and contradictions, however, are individual rather than social in origin. Our attitudes toward sex and family-life are closely bound up with complexities of emotional reaction that have been nurtured since childhood. We have been forced to view sex in a certain fashion, and sex relations have taken on certain forms that are often justified without the least consideration of historical advance or scientific conclusions. From those things that have been touched by a myriad associations, inwrapt in the personality, as it were, by experiences too numerous to recall, it is most difficult to escape. As a result, we can very easily understand the capacity of men and women to dichotomize their approach to reality, focussing a radical lens upon one phase, and a conservative upon another. It is for this reason that many radicals are conservative in sex. All of us want life to move in sharp, simplified patterns, but it does not. That the fundamental changes in contemporary society are outgrowths of our new economic life will be questioned by few. Yet when we consider the aspects of economic change, the manifold ramifications in the structure of society, we find cultural lags, vestigial tendencies, contradictory crisscrossing conceptions that take us far afield often from their fundamental source in order to understand their subtler manifestations.

The world is on the threshold of revolutionary change. In some places, of course, this change is going on faster, and in more sweeping fashion, than in others. This is inevitable. The disintegration of the family, and the decay of the marital institution of the modern world, accompanied by the rise and revolt of youth, are revolutionary developments in our civilization This disintegration and decay, however, as it is part of the purpose of this book to illustrate, are only a phase of a more fundamental revolution that is already tearing at the roots of our social and economic life. Revolutions are not sudden events that fall upon us like an unexpected blast from the dark. No revolution is accomplished by a military guesture, or a legislative decree. A revolution first invades every corner and crevice of life. When conditions necessitate a decisive change, an episode of combat, a brief outburst of struggle, may achieve the topsy-turvying of control that is demanded by the situation. But it is not the episode or the outburst that constitutes the revolution. The revolution has actually occurred long before either the episode or the outburst. These are but an expression of the final turn of the revolution.

There is no endeavor in this book to exaggerate the importance of sex in social life. There is an endeavor, however, to attack the stupid silences that have obscured and distorted its consideration in the past. In the epilogue, this approach has been made clear in a paragraph:

"Our own age is one in which sex monism has become prominent. Sex has become an obsession. This is partly a result of the suppression of all considerations of sex during the last few centuries, and primarily the result of the changes in objective institutions which have accomplished this emancipation from these earlier silences. While sex has been one of the most profound forces in human life, it has not determined social change or economic progress. While its potency may have remained a constant down through the aeons and ages, its influence upon group advance has been secondary rather than primary, negative rather than positive. To many in the contemporary world who are ardent advocates of sex emancipation this observation may appear disappointingly conservative. Our zeal for change, however, should not cause us to lose our sense of equilibrium. We must not challenge sex stupidities by sex exaggerations. Through climatic changes and economic revolutions man has advanced, and his sex life has altered with the variations in existence which have resulted. His sexual customs have oscillated with the movement of external conditions. They have not determined this movement; this movement, on the other hand, has determined them, their form and expression. Sexual ethics, therefore, are more of an effect than a cause in the progress of social relations. They reflect rather than determine the nature of advance."

What we see, then, in the revolution in morals which has occurred in our age is the harbinger of a revolution in social life which is hastening upon us. The old society is in a state of decay. Its old morals have become bankrupt. The new morals are an outgrowth of its rapid disintegration and chaos.

If it seems, as it no doubt will to many, that we have stressed too strongly the importance of the War as a factor in the rise of this new morality, it is because the immediate effect and influence of the War are seldom understood or appreciated. It is not our contention that it was the War that caused this moral chaos. Its origins, on the other hand, are rooted in the rising conflicts and contradictions of Industrial civilization. The economic independence of woman had become a growing reality before the War. The new morality had already started to stir before the War. It was the War, however, that set these forces into rapid rotation. The War itself was created by the same conditions that brought about these other changes. It was a contributing factor, therefore, and not a fundamental. Nevertheless, its direct and immediate influence has been enormous.

The struggle against old and outworn traditions, as we have said, is never a struggle that is fought in one field, or in only one way. The present struggle against the sexual ethics of the older generations is but part of a larger struggle against the older ways of life. Revolt in one field can only be genuinely successful if revolt is also carried into the other fields of life. Moral revolt against an old order can never be secure in its success as long as the old order remains dominant in other forms of existence.

V. F. CALVERTON.

Baltimore, July 2, 1928.

CONTENTS

I THE JAZZ AGE   11

II THE OLD MORALITY   21

III THE SOCIAL BACKGROUND OF OUR MORAL CHAOS   33

IV THE DECAY OF MODERN MARRIAGE   60

V THE NEW MORALITY IN AMERICA   90

VI THE EFFECTS OF CONTRACEPTIVES UPON FEM-
ININE MORALS   119

VII COMPANIONATE MARRIAGE AND THE SEXUAL IM-
PULSE   145

VIII PROSTITUTION AND THE NEW MORALS   167

IX ABORTION AND THE BANKRUPTCY OF THE OLD
MORALS   175

X ILLEGITIMACY AND REVOLT   192

XI THE NEW MORALITY IN GERMANY   207

THE NEW MORALITY IN SOVIET RUSSIA

XII REVOLUTIONARY CHAOS AND CHANGE   223

XIII LOVE, MARRIAGE AND DIVORCE   249

XIV THE ADVANCED ATTITUDE TOWARD BIRTH CON-
TROL AND ABORTION   268

XV PROSTITUTION AND VENEREAL DISEASE   280

XVI THE FUTILE MORALITY OF SOVIET RUSSIA   289

XVII AN EPILOGUE—LOVE AND THE SEX LIFE   305

INDEX   333

THE BANKRUPTCY
OF MARRIAGE

The Bankruptcy of Marriage

THE BANKRUPTCY OF MARRIAGE

CHAPTER I

THE JAZZ AGE

PIROUETTING to the rhythm of the tango, ravaged by the contortions of the Charleston, or, cigarette in hand, shimmeying to the music of the masses, the New Woman and the New Morality have made their theatric debut upon the modern scene. At nights, in the large cities, life spins itself into melodrama. The mad dance of youth, intoxicated with the swell of its new freedom, has encircled the western world. American jazz is almost as popular in London, Berlin, Paris, Riga, and Warsaw as in Chicago and New York. The wild, Corybantian antics of the flapper, flinging herself, in this delirium of escape, night after night upon the edge of nervous ecstasy, are no longer peculiar to our nation. Only in Soviet Russia is this whirligig unfamiliar.

Jazz has become an accepted institution. A leading symphony-conductor contends that it is destined to become a classic. It expresses the spirit of the age.

Youth has steeped itself in its intoxications. Repressions have been released, and in the abandonments of modern life, exhibitionism has changed from a vice into a virtue.

In the flapper we find a vivid symbol of this change. This new girl, with all her emptiness of ideas and effusiveness of emotions, is a revolutionary outgrowth on the feminine scene. She has her counter-part in every country in Europe. She is even allied with the revolt of women in Turkey and feminine insurgents in lands still further removed from western ideas. Her speech, her dress, her gesture are outspoken evidences of the nature of her insurrection. The spread of her influence has been infectious.

In this whirling race of Change, all restraints and restrictions have been sacrificed. The inhibitions once indispensable to feminine virtue have become riddled with scorn. The old sanctity of marriage has been ridiculed by sallies of wit and satire fired at it from every side. Sexual excitements and ecstasies have become experiences to crave and not to constrain. The flapper is consumed by them. Life becomes vivid through their repetition. The old conventions that separated the sexes have been shattered. The old waltz has surrendered to the new jazz. In place of the spinster has sprung up the bachelor girl. She undresses

her mind as well as her body. Instead of hiding her
ankles, she now bares her knees; instead of corseting
her bust, she "v's" her neck. Instead of the old moral
literature, she devours the emancipated new. The literature of today has returned to passion, to a fleshliness that found but faint shadow in the poetry of
Rossetti and the prose of Ruskin. It is a fleshliness
today that dazzles the young by its salacious sentimentalities and melodrama. The emasculated fiction
of previous generations has now become part of a
tradition that has rapidly grown anemic and desic-
cated.

The old family has decayed. The old home has
been replaced by the movie, the club, the dance-hall.
Home has become a place to dine and die. The sentimental hymn of Payne—"There's no place like Home"
has been converted into "There's no place like Home—
Thank God." Carl Marr's picture of the old home,
entitled *Gossip,* which discloses a scene of domestic
quietude and serenity, the women at work at their
spinning wheels, reminds us now of a relic of antiquity.
It is unfamiliar and uninviting, a strange sight that
today has little emotional appeal.

All over the western world it is the same. This new
girl, this modern flapper, with her lack of respect for
the ideals of her predecessors; and this new masculine

youth, with his disregard for the old responsibilities, his disdain for marriage, and contempt for virtue—both were born in the fury of their revolt, in the days of the World War and those that have immediately followed.

The jazz age was born in its tornado of intensity from the vortices of the World War and its aftermath. In recent years its momentum has increased with melodramatic rapidity. Wherever we turn we find its effects scrawled across the face of things. It is part of the chaos of the era.

It is not that the fundamental cause for revolt against the old morals was found in the World War,—it had already begun to stir before the War—but that it took but this catastrophe and its aftermath to set it into rapid rotation.

Then came the War!

In these words are summarized the change and tragedy of an epoch. Their meaning can only be understood in terms of terror and destruction.

The World War not only annihilated the flower of European youth, but it left its deeper effects on the youth that remained, and the generation that grew up with the War as its noisy sentinel. One was occupied in this undertaking, another in that, some were in the midst of careers that promised rich rewards in learning and science; hope tricked itself upon the wings of great inspiration, and men worked for ideals that tradition had approved and hallowed. Then came the War! And all this was shattered. Careers were wrecked, plans broken, and inspiration converted into a brutal war-cry. The ideals for which men fought became mere traffic in the eyes of profiteer and prostitute.

Youth was disillusioned of purpose and aspiration. In Paris the orgy of war-madness transformed the stage into a brothel, with words as mere decoration for gesture and action. The psychosis of the last fling predominated. The imminence of death drove men to the last extremities of desire. Nothing mattered! The theatre responded to their needs. Music halls, cabarets, and amusement resorts had catered to this tendency from the very beginning of the war. Now the theater turned to a kind of sexual insanity in its eagerness to entertain and satisfy the soldier. *La Vie Féminine* attracted enormous audiences night after night and yet even it was surpassed in enthusiastic attendance by Paul Veber's play, *Loute*.[1] Pornography was king of the stage. Everywhere bawdiness was rife.

And the war did not end this!

[1] "The New Spirit in the European Theatre," Huntly Carter.

The European world had been too startled from its equilibrium ever to return to its old routine and ritual. The returning soldiers were not the same men who had once gone to war. They were apprehensive, restless, and disillusioned. The brutalizing terrorism of the war had made these men into maniacs; and it required more than a sudden truce to calm those impulses which this madness of conflict had aroused. The old moral values had lost their influence and power. Bitterness and hatred had become more than occasional emotions in the lives of these men. They had seen their generation "smashed"—as John Freeman, the protagonist in *Fanatics* cried in his attack upon his father and the old generation——

"You who sat here in comfort all these five years of hell. You don't know what I am talking about. You've forgotten, I tell you. . . . Your generation has done ours in. Smashed it! Millions! If we were to stand at that window and they marched past us, they'd march all day, and all night, and all day again for days and nights. Dead men! Dead! For what?"

It was all still a dreadful chimera whose shadow persisted after its substance had flown.

The modern dance was an inevitable outgrowth of this war-madness. Modern youth responded to the wild call. What mattered? To live, to live intensely, to live furiously, to seize from life its every thrill. Such became the new motivation.

In Paris, after the war, they danced. It was the mad, delirious dancing of men and women who had to seize upon something as a vicarious outlet for their crazed emotions. They did not want old opiates that induced sleep and the delusion of a sweet stillness of things and silence. They did not seek the escape which an artificial lassitude brings to minds tormented with worry and pain. They wanted an escape that was active, dynamic, electrical. It had to be an escape that exhilarated, that brought restfulness only from exhaustion. The spirit of tranquillity was alien to the trend of the age.

In the wild, religious fevers of those who danced from city to town and town to city, in that morbid dance of death that animated the high-ways and by-ways of northern Europe over five hundred years ago,[2] one could discover a medieval counterpart of our contemporary jazz-mania. These dancing men and women were dancing the dance of religious lunacy. They would out-dance the devil in their passion for the godliness that might be man's. In the maelstrom of their dancing madness, it was frenzy that became a sign

[2] "Dance of Death"—Hecker.

[17]

of virtue, and hysteria that became the attribute of the pious. The Black Death was upon the earth.

The War was another Black Death that came upon the world. It came in modern and not medieval form. It carried its disease and death into almost every crevice and niche of our civilization.

And it brought with it not the Dance of Death but the Dance of Priapus.

"No flats, no coal, no salt, and no money. Everyone in Paris moans, groans, and grumbles. *But they dance.*" [3]

The western world is mad with this dance. Immediately following the war, endurance contests in the Terpsichorean art became the rage. Individuals and couples danced for hours and hours, with a seemingly interminable zest, all in response to the psychotic undulations of the atmosphere and the environment. It was fever-crazed and frenetic. Every year, every month, the dance takes new forms, assumes new disguises. Each form is more futile than the other. Each change is more sexual. Only the thin division of clothes and the wild cry of the victrola or violin distinguishes the dance from the pageantry of an ancient saturnalia—or the abandonment of the first act in a brothel.

[3] *Daily Mail*, London, Nov. 12, 1919—M. Andree Viollis.

Youth in its revolt has not only turned against the old traditions, but in its search for the new it is dissipating its energies in extravagance and excess. Things serious have too often become greeted *with a sneer*. *Cynicism has become the new faith.* Even in Germany, where the youth movement has more definiteness than in any other country save Soviet Russia, we find this attitude conspicuous. Klaus Mann pictures its chaos in vivid fashion:

"The confusion seems tremendous to me; almost everything seems a question-mark. Which of us can say that he knows clearly the whence and whither of things? But of all things, art has become the questionable.

"Young actors come from their dressing-rooms—not those who are failures and are bitter and disgusted; no, those who are recognized and praised—but still they ask, sadly and hopelessly: Why do we give ourselves? Why are we doing this? And if we should play with all our souls, nobody would be fundamentally interested in our work. What is art today? The young people go to boxing matches and automobile races. When Samson and Breitenstrater have a fight, 16,000 people get excited, but who comes when we play Goethe or Berthold Brecht? The theater will soon close—and besides, one earns more in the movies." [4]

In a later paragraph he adds, with penetrating clarity:

Translated from *Die Neue-Rundschau;* March, 1926.

[19]

"A World War lies between us and our fathers, a sort of revolution. The gods have torn us far apart." [5]

This World War, then, shot into shreds the old ideals, the old morals, the old customs. It is the same in France, the same in England, the same in America.

The Age of Innocence is dead.

[5] *Ibid.*

CHAPTER II

THE OLD MORALITY

THIS new way of life has succeeded only because of the rapid and complete decay of the old. Some adventurous spirits maintain that there is nothing new in this changed form of behavior on the part of our generation, and in a sense they are correct. In the days immediately preceding the fall of Rome there was a flare of freedom in morals that might be cited as example of historical comparison. For a brief time then, the sexual life was disencumbered of the restrictions and regulations that had formerly confined and cramped it, and which afterwards were to bind it into a moral straight-jacket from which it was not to escape until our present age. The period of the Restoration in England in 1660, too, might be suggested as another illustration. In neither of these instances, however, despite the freedom and even license that reigned, was the change as revolutionary as the one we now confront. With the Restoration it was only a segment of society that was affected. Even in Rome the change was not one that raced down to the very roots of existence. In both instances, it was more of an upper-class revolt than one that struck at the very foundations of moral life. The contemporary revolt, on the other hand, is one that has left little of society untouched. The youth of all classes has been shaken. Only the aged have been little disturbed by its influence.

One feature of this revolt that is seldom recognized is that its predominant emphasis is feminine. Girls and women more than boys and men have revolted. Boys and men had taken sex liberties even in the old days, but in a manner that was furtive and clandestine. For the man the revolt has been most sweeping in the destruction of his concepts and ideals. What he did before with slight compunction of conscience, he does now with an intelligent courage. It was the girl and the woman who had refused to yield to the seductions of Eros. Those who succumbed were scorned as immoral and vulgar. A *decent* woman in those days reserved her affections for the marriage-chamber, and if marriage never came heaven alone promised an escape from the uneventful career of a virgin. Today decency has lost its spell. Sophistication has superseded naïveté as a feminine aspiration. Virgins are timid to admit that they are so. Knowledge is more important than innocence—even for women in this modern age.

Where once the man turned to the prostitutes of the cabaret and saloon for his adventures, he now begins to revert to the girl of the more enlightened and emancipated set. The decline in this attraction of the prostitute, which has ensued, was inevitable.

For those of the younger generation it is difficult to understand the enormity of this progress. To them it often does not seem to be a revolution at all. In order to appreciate how portentous has been this change, how profound this transvaluation of values, it is important for us to understand the old morals which the women of the last century observed.

Let us turn back to the America of almost a hundred years ago. One of the most interesting pictures of this country at that time was done by the mother of the famous Trollope family, Frances M. Trollope. Mrs. Trollope, who in the last twenty-six years of her life dedicated her talent to the composition of one hundred and fourteen books, of which the overwhelming majority were novels, lived in the United States during the early years of Jackson's first administration. Her stay in America extended over a period of three years. It was in her book "The Domestic Manners of the

Americans" that she gathered together her impressions of this country and its people. Few books about America are so delightfully vivacious, so refreshingly candid and so intimate in their descriptions of the American mores. It was in the depiction of American manners and social life that she excelled. In this picture of American ladies of the last century, she has given us a humorous and yet not distorted description of the old morality:

"At Cincinnati there is a garden where the people go to eat ices, and to look at roses. For the preservation of the flowers, there is placed at the end of one of the walks a sign-post sort of daub, representing a Swiss peasant girl, holding in her hand a scroll, requesting that the roses might not be gathered. Unhappily for the artist, or for the proprietor, or for both, the petticoat of this figure was so short as to show her ankles. The ladies saw, and shuddered; and it was formally intimated to the proprietor that if he wished for the patronage of the ladies of Cincinnati, he must have the petticoat of this figure lengthened. The affrighted purveyor of ices sent off an express for the artist and his paint pot. He came, but unluckily not provided with any color that would match the petticoat; the necessity, however, was too urgent for delay, and a flounce of blue was added to the petticoat of red, giving bright and shining evidence before all men, of the immaculate delicacy of the Cincinnati ladies."

Again, in suggesting a picnic to a young American lady, Mrs. Trollope records the reply as typical:

"I fear you will not succeed; we are not used to such sort of things here, and I know it is considered very indelicate for ladies and gentlemen to sit down together on the grass."

A few other episodes are not less characteristic:

"A young German gentleman of perfectly good manners, once came to me greatly chagrined at having offended one of the principal families in the neighborhood, by having pronounced the word *corset* before the ladies of it. An old female friend had kindly overcome her own feelings so far as to mention to him the cause of the coolness he had remarked, and strongly advised his making an apology. He told me that he was perfectly well disposed to do so, but felt himself greatly at a loss how to word it."

"An English lady who had long kept a fashionable boarding-school in one of the Atlantic cities, told me that one of her earliest cares with every newcomer was the endeavor to substitute real delicacy for this affected precision of manner; among many anecdotes she told me one of a young lady about fourteen, who on entering the receiving room, where she only expected to find a lady who had inquired for her, and seeing a young man with her, put her hands before her eyes, and ran out of the room again, screaming, 'A man! a man! a man!'"

Such illustrations of American attitudes and manners could be multiplied almost endlessly by reference to the literature of the last century. In fact, one has but to study the changes in dress that have been ac-

complished in the generations that divide those of the
old era from the contemporary, in order to apprehend
the nature of this revolution in manners and morals.
The fashions of 1850 and those of 1920, the long
dress and the short dress, the hoop-skirt and the latest
achievements in knickers, represent more than a revelation in sartorial contrasts. They signify an entire
change in moral attitudes. The bustle skirt and the
"leg of mutton" sleeve are as indisputably a part of
the paraphernalia of a dead age as are the stage coach
and the horse tram. Along with their passing has disappeared the type of woman and the character of
morals with which they have been associated.

In Victorian England, despite Mrs. Trollope's amusing animadversions upon the prudity of American women, a similar attitude prevailed. The woman was
trained to consider freedom as a vice, and ambition
as the sin of the man. While the women of the proletariat toiled from sunrise to sundown, the ladies of the
leisure class were cultivated to move within a world
glassed-in from the merciless realities that gave them
their wealth. Ignorance was their main protection from
evil. The "clinging vine" type of woman was the popular ideal. It was the clinging weakness, the sweet submission of "strictly feminine deportment" that Mrs.
Sandford, expressing her age in her book "Woman."

exalted with such childish conviction. "Nothing is so likely to conciliate the affection of the other sex," she wrote, "as a feeling that women look to them for guidance and support." In the States, Mrs. A. J. Graves, in language even more specific, expressed the same sentiments. Her book, "Woman in America," which appeared under the imprint of Harper Brothers in 1858, purported to be "an examination into the moral and intellectual condition of American female society." Her words are expressive of the attitude that prevailed:

"The supremacy of the husband as the head of the family institution is similar to the supremacy of the governing power in a state, and there is the like obligation to obedience in both.

"She is required, therefore, not only to submit to man as her head in the marriage relation but she must not assume to herself any rights of participation with him in the management or control of civil or political affairs.

"She (a good woman) has no desire to rule where she feels it to be her duty, as it is her highest pleasure 'to love, honor and obey'; and she submits with cheerful acquiescence to that order in the conjugal relation which God and nature have established.

"Woman feels she is not made for command, and finds her truest happiness in submitting to those who wield a rightful sceptre in justice, mercy and love."

In fine, innocence on the part of woman, in those times, was preferable to wisdom. The sentiment expressed by Sir Willoughy in Meredith's novel "The Egoist," in his desire to have his bride "come to him out of an egg-shell, somewhat more astonished at things than a chicken, but as completely enclosed before he tapped the shell, and seeing him with her sex's eyes first of all men," is strikingly illustrative of the kind of woman man desired during the age of the viceless Victorians. "We have our faults," wrote James Runciman in his interesting essay on "Public and Private Morality" [1] "crimes and vice flourish; but from the Court down to the simplest middle-class society in our provincial towns, the spread of seemliness and purity is distinctly marked . . . . . Can any creature be more dainty, more sweet, more pure, than the ordinary English girl of today?"

It must be remembered that this dainty, sweet, pure, English girl was but part of an entire culture that made of purity a passion and sweetness a touchstone of feminine virtue. Her dress, her manner, her speech, her literature, all photographed this fact. She walked in a world that was almost as confined as the boundaries of a nunnery. The words of literature had to be chosen to suit the innocence of her nature. Thomas

---

[1] "Sidelights."

Hardy's novels, for example, were annoyingly realistic and indelicate. Leslie Stephen had to advise Hardy, when "The Hand of Ethelberta" was about to be published in the *Cornhill Magazine,* of which Stephen was then the editor, that he should not portray a lady as "amorous" but "sentimental." "Oliver Twist" was attacked because it was concerned with the "outcasts of humanity" and because "by such publications the happy ignorance of innocence is degraded." This criticism is a marvelously precise picture of the spirit of the age. "Our youth," the review continued, "should not even suspect the possibility of such hidden depths of guilt." In other words they should live as if evil were a fiction, and innocence were the essence of life. In pursuit of this puritanical ideal Rossetti's lavender passions had been condemned as unashamed depravity, and Swinburne's "Poems and Ballads" and Fielding's "Tom Jones" had been burned upon a public pyre. Ibsen's "Ghosts" had been attacked in 1890 as a menace to virtue, and the theater in which it was staged in England threatened with suit as a "disorderly house." It is no wonder, then, that Thackeray confessed that "since the author of 'Tom Jones' was buried, no writer of fiction among us has been permitted to depict to his utmost power a Man. We must drape him, and give him a certain conventional simper. Society will not tolerate the Natural in Art."

Harriet Martineau's comment upon the coronation of Queen Victoria as being an "occasion (I believe the only one) on which a lady could be alone in public without an escort" seems absurd today only when we fail to think of the other moral trappings of the era. Revered but without rights, this nineteenth century woman was dependent upon her husband for her existence. "The actual bond-servant of her husband, no less so far as legal obligations (go) than slaves so-called," John Stuart Mill wrote, "she owed a life-long obedience to him at the altar, and is held to it all through her life by law." The husband could sell, lease, or mortgage without his wife's consent any property he received from her at marriage. The husband could appropriate any balance standing in her name at her banker's. The husband could get a complete divorce and remarry if he proved his wife unfaithful, but for the wife to secure a divorce, adultery was insufficient. Other elements, cruelty, desertion, or the like were needed in addition to adultery to justify the woman's case. And in all matters concerning the children the father was in the eyes of the English law the rightful guardian who could take them out of the woman's care at his own discretion.

To leave this society, with such conventions and standards, and enter our own, is to many a plunge from order into chaos. Where before woman's place was definite and limited to certain bounds, it is now indefinite and well-nigh boundless. At one time woman knew her place, as the reactionary is wont to contend, and that place, being sharply circumscribed, assured a certain orderliness in feminine behavior. Today woman is to be found in every place. Her domain is no longer only the home. Her behavior, therefore, has become as various as her inclinations. She has not only acquired more rights, won a legal and political status, and severed the conventions of the narrow world in which she had been formerly confined, but, with her growing economic independence, she has seized upon those privileges which once were the sole possession of men.

Woman's emergence into this wider world has meant, thus, a rapid change in her entire outlook upon life. The revolt has been at once volcanic and profound. Beginning with change in her economic existence, it changed her dress, her manners, her morals, her ideals.

Since the War this revolution in moral values has advanced at a maddening gallop. Defiance has now inspirited its challenge. Where before there had only been revolt against the old, there is now a creative desire for the new. The new Woman of yesterday is hardly able to keep pace with the new Youth of today. The new morality of which she is a dynamic expression is already fumbling for form. The young have greeted it with a spontaneity that is irresistible. For them it seems the dawn of a new freedom.

CHAPTER III

THE SOCIAL BACKGROUND OF OUR MORAL CHAOS

I

HERE we have a new morality and a new woman, and a world that in so many ways is changed in appearance and ideal. These newnesses belong to a new age. A new age, however, does not burst upon us with the unanticipated treachery of a typhoon, sweeping all before it with its suddenness. It is only its external manifestations that sometimes dart upon us unawares, and with a strange violence. Its underlying forms are often of old duration.

The question—how did we get this way—is, therefore one of very intricate and complicated character. The World War, after all, was in itself but a sharp climax in the career of modern industrial civilization. It gave rise to a number of forces that otherwise might have taken much longer to acquire their present momentum. The old morals had begun to decay before the war; it was the War, however, that chalked a turning-point in the disintegration of the ethics and ideals of the

ruling class. The economic rise of woman had occurred before the War also; it was the War, nevertheless, that inspired this rise with a sharp spurt and made
it take on more gigantic proportions. Behind it all,
of course, *as the fundamental cause of the changes
that we have recorded, is the development of the machine age and industrial civilization.* Industrialism
brought with it the factory-system of production with
mass-economics as its main manifestation; it drew women into industry, destroyed the unity of the home,
and brought the family to a rapid ruin. It brought
a new social class into power, the bourgeoisie, which
spent its energies in first promoting a morality in consonance with its earlier life, and which later, through
changes in its own existence, came to disregard this
morality in practice. The economic independence of
woman was made possible through the advance of industry, and the expansion of this new ruling class.
The War resulted from the inescapable conflicts in economic life which had been created by this industrial
system.

What we see, then, is the operation of a multiple of
factors which have all grown out of the conflict and
chaos of industrial civilization. The fundamental
cause of this change, it can be said, therefore, is industrial. The economic independence of woman and the

decay in the morality of the bourgeois class and the World War, when all is said, *are but derivatives of this basic revolution in economic life.* The new morality, with its changed sex attitude, is but one of its newest forms.

2

The economic independence of woman arose side by side with the decay in bourgeois mores. Both sprang from the economic existence stimulated by the Industrial Revolution. Economic independence soon brought about moral independence. The clinging vine type of girl and the submissive type of mother, apostrophized in song and celebrated in sermon, have become obsolescent. Woman's demands for equal rights with man have extended to the sexual sphere as well as to the social. The invention of contraceptives, as we shall see in a later chapter, has fortified her independence as a sexual being, and given her an opportunity for a sex life that is no more handicapped than that of man. With economic freedom there is no need for the surrender of her rights to a morality prescribed for her by man. As long as she owed her livelihood to man, she owed him her virtue. It was a debt that was obvious and unavoidable. *With the gradual disappearance of this economic dependence, the necessity for moral subjection, was no longer urgent.* Liberty to live her life as she pleased, in terms of equality of privilege, now became possible for her after centuries of moral enslavement. This meant revolt against the home, the family, and the rigorous demands of domestic life and virtue.

The Industrial Revolution forced women out of the old ways of life. Industry sucked her into the vortices of a machine-driven world. It destroyed her position as homemaker and crippled her capacity as a mother. At first her lack of skill and talent exposed her to the most abject enslavement. As her presence in industry continued, however, skill was acquired and her assertiveness became manifest in woman's organizations and trade unions. With the growth of education among her sex, she undertook vaster tasks in the economic and industrial world. Eventually women of all classes were drawn into economic endeavor. From the quiet submissive housewife she has now become active as factory worker, vocational adviser, stenographer, teacher, politician, orator, preacher, lawyer, doctor, and in fact, has entered into almost every occupation undertaken by men. This change from the static life of a mother into the dynamic life of worker revolutionized her entire outlook upon existence. It effected the feminine revolt against masculine oppression in economics, politics, education and morals.

The expression of this revolt, however, in active, vivid and definite form, was aided by the general chaos of the era. If it had not been for the destruction of the old ideals, the disintegration of the old morals, the cataclysm of the War, and the confusion of the age, with cynicism as its philosophic embodiment, the rising economic independence of women might not have included morals within its immediate range of protest and insurrection. In other words, there might have been a "cultural lag," that would have constrained women to accept revolt in morals less rapidly than in economic and political life. The tendency, particularly in the case of reactions pertaining to the sexual, is toward the continuance of habits for a long time after their actual cause has disappeared. In fine, woman might have continued to observe the old morality in which her dependence was conspicuous, even though her economic independence was already achieved. Such persistence of habit, and contradiction of relationships, is not at all unusual or uncommon. Eventually, of course, it would have been solved by the attainment of mutual independence in morals as well as in economics. This solution, however, might have been painfully slow in arrival. The presence of these numerous contributing factors, to be sure, prevented this tardiness in the evolution of a moral parallel.

With a world disorganized, its ideals shattered, its body bleeding with the ravages of war, revolt on the part of women already in revolt in other fields did not experience delay. Indeed, these conditions of social chaos inspired this revolt with early courage and conviction. It plunged headlong into this new freedom which has already become characteristic of our age.

3

Now let us consider several of the changes in terms of their historical evolution in order to see how the old moral attitude had grown into an ethic, and the new moral attitude crystallized into revolt against it.

With the growth of commercialism in the fifteenth century, the exploration of the world, the development of trade routes and the discovery of America, the merchant or bourgeois class rapidly rose into the position of supremacy in the modern world. The rise of this bourgeois class signified the decadence of the aristocracy and the economic system which had prevailed during the days of feudalism. It was not until the seventeenth century in England, however, that this bourgeoisie really came into control of things. The eighteenth century marked the introduction of a profound and permanent change into the administration of social and moral life. This change was conspicu-.

ously reflected in morals. The purity which is known sometimes as prudery and at others as puritanism is one of its emanations. It expressed itself in the conventions of literature as well as in those of dress.

The story of changing customs in clothes, as we indicated in the first chapter, is a long and revealing story in itself. We can but note a few of its developments in this analysis. In this advance from an aristocratic to a bourgeois culture, several changes are at once obvious and signal.[1] The old dress of the aristocracy had been characterized by extravagance and those excesses of adornment which can be attributed to the vanities of self-indulgence. Ornament was profuse. "Take from them their periwigs, their paintings, their jewels, their rowles, their bolsterings," wrote Lyly in "Euphues," "and thou shalt soon perceive that a woman is the least part of herself ... Look in their closets, and there shalt thou find an apothecary's shop of sweet confections, a surgeon's box of sundry salves, a pedlar's pack of new fangles." Women then also knew the art of bodily display which so many imagine she has only learned to acquire in this recent generation. The tempting disclosure of the soft curves of the breasts was more ravishingly accomplished by

[1] For fuller treatment of these changes in general life and cultural concepts, see the author's "Sex Expression in Literature."

the women of this period than by those of the modern. The paintings of the era do justice to this sartorial device. All of this changed, however, with the rise of this new social class. Addison, for example, in the eighteenth century, attacked severely this tendency which, in his opinion, belonged exclusively to his immoral predecessors. Writing in *The Guardian,* under the title of "Naked Bosoms," he declared that:

"The clergy of the present age are not transported with these indiscreet fervors (dress reform among women). . . . For this reason, I look upon myself to be of great use to these good men; while they are employed in extirpating mortal sins and crimes of a higher nature, I should be glad to rally the world out of indecencies and venial transgressions.

"Thus much I thought fit to premise before I resume the subject which I have already handled, I mean the naked bosoms of our British ladies. I hope they will not take it ill of me, if I still beg that they will be covered."

Even the dress of men changed. These Puritans were not called Roundheads without reason. They shaved their heads in order to achieve a simplicity of appearance. Their women adopted an attire barren of costliness or beauty. Dress that inspired sensual desire was condemned as satanic. Extravagance was execrated. Religion which once had smiled so sweetly upon the old habits of the aristocracy, was now made to frown upon that life as one of wickedness and vice.

This new moral attitude came with a new economic life. The changes in dress thus resulted from the changes in social outlook and economic existence. The old aristocracies had been a thriftless, extravagant class, given to the adoration of the useless. Clothes had been fashioned more for tinsel and filigree than for covering the body. This class did not work, but had the rest of society to work for it. Consequently it never came to regard thrift as a virtue, or labor as a function of importance in life. Labor was degradation. Labor was for the serfs and townsmen, the merchants and manufacturers—in other words, the lower orders of society. Its gaudiness of dress like the license of its life, therefore, reflected the environment that conditioned its existence. This new social class, however, the bourgeoisie, arose from a different economic milieu. It was a working class. It knew the significance of parsimony. Thrift was its cardinal virtue. Even its religion was economical. Its pastor, Richard Steele, maintained that "success in business is proof that a man has labored faithfully in his vocation, and that God has blessed his trade," and another of its ecclesiastics, Baxter, taught that "prudence and piety are the best of friends." Its plainness of dress, as a consequence, was a product of its economic philosophy. It could not afford the excrescences that were exquisite but useless. Utility was its criterion. Beauty could only be genuine when it was useful. Even in religion that same parsimony of purpose intruded. The churches were not to be embellished with the trappings of pagan artistry or papal magnificence. Everything was simple, plain and economical.

The morals of this class were, therefore, based upon a studied economy. While at first the theater was banned, it was later purified and converted into an auditorium for moral instruction. Literature was castrated of all charms except the conventional. Adultery which had been the enticing theme of Restoration drama was never mentioned except in a whisper of condemnation. The family became the exalted center of moral virtue. Love must be lawful—otherwise it is libidinous. Chastity became the essence of feminine virtue. This was all part of the property-concept of morality which had grown out of the economic life of the bourgeoisie. The woman became extolled in words, but in fact was valued merely as a property possession. Chastity was an excellent protection to the propertied attitude.[2] As Samuel Johnson remarked, "the chastity

[2] For further consideration of several points in this chapter, see the author's "Sex Expression in Literature."

of women being of the utmost importance, as all property depends upon it, they who forfeit it should not have any possibility of being restored to good character." [3]

All the life of the eighteenth and nineteenth centuries in England, for instance, was dedicated to these ideals. When we speak of morality even today it is in terms of its comparison with these mores of the bourgeois class. If a thing is said to be immoral, it is usually understood as being a deviation from, or a revolt against, this attitude that we have just described. Instead of conceiving of morality as a relative thing, differing among different peoples and at different times in the history of the same people, we have made of this particular code which we have known in the last two centuries, the criterion of "morality."

Into the literature of these two centuries, bourgeois morality introduced itself in dictatorial form. In fact, it was the dictatorship of the bourgeoisie in art. Artists were consecrated to moral virtue. Susan Ferrier thought "the only good purpose of a book was to inculcate morality and convey some lesson of instruction as well as delight," and Jane Austen insisted that she would "let other pens dwell on guilt and misery," and asserted her eagerness to "quit such odious subjects"

[3] Quoted from John Langdon-Davies' "Short History of Women."

in order to "restore everybody, not greatly in fault with themselves, to tolerable comfort, and to have done with all the rest."

The young men were brought up consequently in the spirit of this old morality which we pictured in the first chapter of this book. This morality which we now call "old," as we have seen, was, in the eighteenth century "new." It was then a morality in revolt against the ethics of the landed aristocracy. The morality of the aristocracy one then would have called the "old" morality, and the morality of the rising bourgeoisie would have been called the "new."

Since that time the new has become old, and a newer morality has arisen. Everywhere the old morality is challenged.

One of the important factors that has undermined this old ethics has been the great change that has taken place in the attitude of the bourgeoisie. Not that the private-property concept has become less pervasive, but that its ethics, under the influence of new conditions, has lost its former asceticism and rigor. The bourgeoisie was a moral class—that is, moral in terms of its original morality. Now it is not. Only the petty bourgeoisie is moral in this sense of the word. The causes of this change are obvious. In the first place, as we have said, the bourgeoisie was originally a work-

ing class. It did not have a leisure-class attitude. In
fact it condemned a leisure-class attitude. Today this
has altered. The bourgeoisie who now represent our
plutocracy constitute a leisure class. Prosperity has
brought us to the billionaire epoch. In the eighteenth
century the ruling bourgeois groups had preserved a
morality necessary to their survival; from this morality developed these moral concepts which still linger
but do not bind. With the centralization of capital, the
acceleration of production, and the achievement of ab-
sentee-ownership of industry, combined with the inheritance of wealth which frees the larger part of the
younger members of this group also from the necessity of toil, a leisure class was an inevitable result. The
bourgeois mores, the old morality that is, was never
made for a leisure-class ethic. It was an ethic that
grew out of hard and trying struggle, an ethic in which
asceticism was a virtue and diversion a sin. But a
leisure class cannot live upon asceticism, nor exist without diversion. This contradiction had but one solution.
The old morals had to crack and crumble. And so
they have. The upper bourgeoisie, from the point of
view of bourgeois morality, is the most immoral class
upon the earth. This fact is to be observed everywhere, in divorce-scandals, court trials, newspaper
disclosures, and in the novels and dramas devoted to

the upper set. It was this class, we must remember; that once directed, by example as much as by precept, the moral destiny of millions. Today the precepts remain but the example has vanished. Practice contradicts precept.

It is only the petty-bourgeoisie, or the lower and poorer middle-class, that still endeavors to observe the old morality in practice—and even with the petty bourgeoisie it is only the older and not the newer generation that is at all rigid in its restrictions. The proletariat by the very nature of its labor and the disintegration of its family by the demands of industrial production, could never have observed, in any strict sense, the dictates of bourgeois morality. If the mother was moral, in the bourgeois sense of the word, it was as much on account of necessity as choice; if the father was moral it was an anomaly. It is only when proletarians become bourgeoisified that they crusade in favor of virtue. After all, the proletariat had to provide the prostitute.

Today the young generation, among all classes, is in revolt.

To be sure, the contradiction between moral precept and moral practice among the upper-bourgeoisie was only one of the factors that destroyed the ideals of their world. While it had set into motion a number of changes that had been gradually undermining the structure of this morality, the magic of motto and slogan did not rapidly lose its inveigling appeal and inspiration. Youth still could be captured by words that promised kingdoms which reality denied. The contradiction between the magic of words and the logic of action was to be realized only after a great catastrophe and a terrible chaos.

The World War disclosed that contradiction. A war of economic imperialisms became a "war for democracy"; a struggle among greedy nations for control of economic markets became a struggle "to make the world a better place to live in"; a war that was to prepare for more and greater wars was called "a war to end war." The promise of world peace through the institution of a League of Nations has become an experience of world chaos supervised by a League of Rogues.

Millions had to die in order to teach the multitude the emptiness of words. These words had stood for the old ideals. Pre-war civilization had believed in these words. This civilization had brought on this war. These words became hollow mockery that could not hide the disaster and death they had caused. The ideals they had represented became mere sham and deception. They had buried idealism instead of in-

spiring it. They had sacrificed life instead of saving
it. They had been mere will-o'-wisps that had led men
to destruction.

Our age is one of change and revolution. We are
at the dawn of either a great catastrophe or a great
renaissance. Our life has quickened. We live at a
convulsive fever heat, our pulse-beat accelerated, our
nerves at incessant tension, as the mad race of civilization dashes us along its ever-thinning precipice. The
appalling signs of decay fence in our vision in every
latitude. Our social and philosophic literature has already begun the swan-song of our era.

In "The Decline of the West," Spengler predicts the
end of our civilization. Keyserling in his "Travel
Diary of a Philosopher" exalts the exotic, and discovers
in the black continent "the greatest creative power in
the world." H. G. Wells in his autobiographical novel
"The World of William Clissold," maintains that our
social system is on the edge of vertigo. In "Icarus,"
Bertrand Russell describes the future of man and science as dismal and ominous. Wyndham Lewis in his
"Art of Being Ruled" reiterates the same criticism.
Science, he asserts, "in its present vulgarized condition
. . . . represents simply the principle of destruction; it
is more deadly than a thousand plagues, and every day
we perfect it, or our popularly industrially applied ver-

sion of it." In America even Waldo Frank, aghast at
this spectacle of human chaos and world calamity avers
that "we are decomposing because the experimental
assumptions that held our culture together are on the
wane . . . . our spiritual body is breaking up."

This state of our world, reflected in the critical literature of our age, is forced upon us in vivid and embarrassing detail in the economic and political crises of
our post-bellum existence. War has become an imminent menace. In newspaper, magazine and book it
has become an ubiquitous, consuming topic. Discussions of it range over an enormity of phenomena. The
work of Barnes, Ewart, Fabre-Luce, Fay, Demartial,
Monteglas, and John Kenneth Turner confined largely
to the problem of war guilt is but one phase of the
interest. In "The Origin of the Next War" Bakeless
subjects our present civilization to a disturbing analysis. While Spengler, H. G. Wells, Bertrand Russell,
Wyndham Lewis, and Waldo Frank announce the
downfall of our supremacy, their criticisms are essentially philosophical. Mr. Bakeless, like Mr. Barnes,
and the newer school of historians, approaches the
problem of the modern world without the delay of picturesque phrase or the evasion of vaporous speculation.
Their interest is with the distinctly concrete and practical. Ever since Philip Gibbs, in 1920, let fall his

sentimental bombshell, "Now It Can Be Told," and
Nitti, in "The Decadence of Europe," punctured the
myth of Gallic purity and perfection, the attitude of
our generation has been prepared for the disclosures
of economic conflict and individual duplicity that lay
behind the World War. In "The Genesis of the World
War" Barnes revealed the chicanery of individual motive in the problem of war guilt, but, it must be admitted, the importance of where the war guilt rests, in
the final analysis, is far less fundamental than the nature of the social system that produces its nefarious
diplomacy, fructifies its destructive ambitions. Bakeless is concerned with the economic struggle behind all
modern wars, the struggle that plunged the world into
the great chaos of 1914, and the struggle that at present is threatening to foment a similiar cataclysm.

"The war to end war failed, and forces identical with
those that caused the last World War are actively at work
today, preparing the way for a new one," writes Mr. Bakeless, and then adds, that though "an uneasy consciousness
that this is so prevails pretty generally, the facts have not
hitherto been frankly faced."

What are the facts that have confronted us since
1918?

The attacks upon Soviet Russia that followed the
Armistice of 1918, the terrible conflict between Russia

and Poland, which lasted from 1918 to 1921; the three
years' war which ended with surrender of Greek ambitions in Smyrna in 1922; the Egyptian revolt against
the British in 1919; the invasion of the Poles in Gal-
licia and of the Afghans into India; the battles between
the French and Turks, the Italians and Albanians; the
march of the Roumanians into Hungary; the communist revolt in South Africa in 1922; the clashes in China;
the Lithuanian seizure of Memel; the bombardment
of Corfu by the Italians; the unsuccessful revolts in
Brazil and Georgia; the Moroccan set-to of 1925—
all these are but part of the manifestations of unrest
and agitation that are seething in our post-bellum civilization. The threat of another World War in 1921,
for instance, when Great Britain and Turkey were in
ferocious dispute, was saved from realization only by
the protest of the British colonies. Even worse than
the actual conflicts, however, are the incentives to
further conflicts. The Versailles Treaty, of course, in
a superficial way, is responsible for the greater part
of the political friction that exists in the European
situation. Yet the existence of a score of other factors
resulting from the fluctuating economic rivalries of
nations is more fundamental.

John Carter in "Man is War" contends that "war is
inherent in the Atlantic way of life," and with the in-

anity of a Southern gentleman defends the virtues of belligerency and primitivism. Haldane in "Callinicus" proves the superiority of chemical warfare to mechanical, and, indeed, urges its humaneness as a form of annihilation. In "Paris," Fuller pictures the martial tactics of the coming age. In the meantime, England, in anticipation of approaching difficulty, builds up a military base at Singapore; France maintains an army larger than Germany's before the war; Italy announces its program of future expansion—and the United States increases its armaments, organizes training camps for military diversion, and provides college manuals for instruction in the fine art of murder.

The realities that confront us at present, nevertheless, are but minor compared with those that indelibly pencil themselves in shadowy and forbidding grotesque upon the face of the future. The disaster of our civilization is economic. While for those with a flare for things derivative of essences and elixirs, or easily enchanted by the mystical, the catastrophe may be spiritual, there is only to be said that the emptiness of spirituality and the destiny-determining power of economics have been attested by the holocaust of the teens. The machine-age is driving us to social paranoia. This fact is illustrated in mild detail by the number of articles and books that are appearing in protest against the dangers of imperialism and the tragedy of waste. In the early philippics of Pettigrew and the more recent work of Nearing, Dunn, Barnes, Knight, Jenke, and others, the nature of American imperialism has been given extensive delineation. In "The People's Corporation" a millionaire liberal attacks the anarchy and inefficiency of production that our world has accepted with such a complacent Cheshire grin. In "The Tragedy of Waste" Stuart Chase indicts the entire organization of our economic system. In "Profits" Catchings and Foster point out the source of our evil, the incapacity of the producers to consume what they produce because of the insufficiency of their wage. If we turn to radical literature, the revelations are more fundamental. Every piece of socialist and communist literature, from Sidney and Beatrice Webb's "Decay of Capitalist Civilization" to Bukharin's "Historical Materialism" and Trotsky's "Whither England," contains a diagnosis of the economic decay of contemporary society.

Our youth thus has been driven to what may be called our Idealless Age. Ideals are thought of as abstractions that confuse rather than clarify by their inspiration. Truth, love, beauty, goodness, peace, are examples of ideals with which men have charged their faith and to which they have dedicated their intelligence. They are concepts super-imposed upon an imaginary world. Faith in an after-world, or the attitude of other-worldliness, for instance, is an excellent though extreme example of an ideal. Men have fought, suffered, and died for it. Religions have preached love and stressed virtue for hundreds of years. Philosophers have taught goodness and exalted peace for untold generations. Hearts have leaped at the flash of a symbol, beat with mad haste at the cry of a motto, and expired at the barricade for an ideal. Sacrifice has been unwearying, but the struggle—futile. Such has been the history of idealism.

The eighteenth century was resonant with new salutations. The fever of a new philosophy had seized the public like a spreading infection. The social philosophy of feudalism was corrupt and putrescent. The revolutionary philosophy of the bourgeoisie rose like a banner of aspiration amid the ruins of an aristocratic society. Men spoke of Natural Law, Equity, Justice, Liberty and Truth with the fervor of enthusiasts and fanatics. They became social superstitions. Into gardening, architecture, literature, philosophy, these new attitudes penetrated. The very atmosphere seemed to breathe the spirit of revolution. These ideals, these heaven-promising phrases, these magnificent calls to arms, were but the inspiration of dreams that outran realities. Man had learned to protest and to denounce, to hate, and to destroy, but he had not yet learned the nature of reconstruction. He had not yet learned the nature of his environment. He had not yet learned that to mouth phrases is not to change economic destiny. All of the glorious faith of Helvetius, Rousseau, D'Holbach, Condorcet, Diderot—faith in environment and the possibilities of change and progress—were but part of a great movement that was to give birth to nothing more than the bourgeois societies of the nineteenth century. In the eyes of Morellet, who saw the era of early insurrection, witnessed the Revolution, lived through the Napoleonic triumphs, and survived the coup d'état of the thirties, the spectacle was one of torn and tortured disillusionment.

The morbidity of the Weltschmerz school, the morbidity of the Byronites, clouded a generation. It was the literary echo of this period of disillusionment.

But men still trusted in ideals. If they were no longer the ideals of the revolution, no longer the faith in rapid change and illimitable progress, they were the ideals of religious hope and moral redintegration. After Waterloo the European world was flattered with a placidity of feature that was as beguiling as it was capricious. The revolutions in France, the difficulty in Crimea, the Franco-Prussian festivity, the Commune

—were all affairs at once episodic and brief. People no longer lived in camps, and bore their childen en route to new battles as they had in the Thirty Years' War, nor did they encompass continents in their clamor for empire or worship of a military champion. Industrial progress became unprecedented. Economic expansion became a national aspiration of gigantic and ferocious proportions. Advanced methods of transportation created a world genuflecting to the rule of the new industrialists. Imperialism clothed itself in the guise of benevolence and religion. Mutability prevailed. Browning's enthusiasm burst into the immortal absurdity:

> "God's in his Heaven,
> All's right with the world."

and Tennyson, surrounded by idyl and dream, sang of the "parliament of man." If James Thomson, with his "City of Dreadful Night," Thomas Beddoes with his suicide as a fitting climax to the heroics of his verse, and Algernon Swinburne with his eroticism and narcomania, represent deviation, its influence upon the spirit of the age was no more marked than Samuel Butler's influence upon the morals of the era.

It was not Butler's cynicism, but Tennyson's idealism, that prevailed.

Even in the attacks upon the Victorian Weltgeist,

the motive was idealistic. While Dickens and Thackeray were content with satirizing deceit and hypocrisy, George Eliot exalted the spirit of a freer ethic. Despite her audacious fleer at convention, however, her preachments were inevitably permeated with idealism. It was the stern voice of duty that she emphasized. Duty was an abstraction that awed and inspired. Its relativity did not dismay the Victorian moralists. In the criticism of Ruskin, who gave Pre-Raphaelitism its "one white wing of moral purpose," was the same idealistic substance. His denunciations of the money-changers were always ethical. His eloquence was invariably that of ethical indignation. Economics and ethics became synonymous sciences. Even in the diatribes of Carlyle, as in the proletarian polemics of Thomas Cooper, there was this same sweep of moral fervor. It was cupidity that they assailed. Carlyle was a modern Jeremiah deriding an ancient vice. Yet with all his contempt for his age, his fiery assaults upon its doctrines and ethics, he was fundamentally an idealist. Like Ruskin, he stressed ideals. He battled with his contemporaries because they failed to uphold his ideals. Cant and hypocrisy were his great targets. His premises were no less fatuous than those of the eighteenth century utopians. His understanding of economic causation was culpably superficial.

And so out of this chaos of change and catastrophe we have come to scorn the ideals of love, truth, justice. Youth sneers at ideals. It prefers cynicism. What are these words—men cry. You cannot deceive us with them again—is the inevitable declaration. A stirring part of an old culture, they have become but sentimental vestiges withering upon the carapace of the new. We have become sick of preachments and abstractions, sceptical of word and gesture. Through idealism, men have been tricked by phrase and ruined by aspiration. Energy has been wasted upon the hopeless and futile.

For centuries Christianity has preached love without striving to change the social forces that made love impossible. It is not for us, like Carlyle and Ruskin, to upbraid the money-merchants, preach peace and condemn avarice, but to endeavor to change the economic structure of our society which creates money-merchants, thwarts peace and encourages avarice. Exhortation is ineffectual. Peace societies are a blur upon modern intelligence—they foster war by their ignorance.

"We may desire abolition of war, industrial justice, greater equity of opportunity for all. *But no amount of preaching good-will or the golden rule or cultivation of sentiments of love and equity will accomplish the results.* There must be change in objective arrangements and institutions. *We must work on the environment, not merely on the hearts of men.* To think otherwise is to suppose that flowers can be raised in a desert or motor cars run in a jungle. Both things can happen and without a miracle. But only by first changing the jungle and the desert." [4] (Italics mine.)

[4] John Dewey—"Reconstruction in Philosophy."

CHAPTER IV

THE DECAY OF MODERN MARRIAGE

I.

THE obvious and immediate result of this chaos in moral life has been the rapid disintegration and decay of marriage as a social institution. This decay is not a subtle, concealed change that fails to betray itself to the public vision. It is a phenomenon manifest even to the reactionary. Institutions, it must be remembered, do not snap and fall upon us in the sudden, sharp fashion of a wind-storm. Their disintegration is more gradual, and it is only at the moment of actual collapse that the process assumes the nature of violence. The marital conception which we have known is now passing through a period of fast change and swift decay.

The release of the new morals is closely connected with the fading of the old conception of marriage. Monogamous marriage is based upon the idea of a lifetime relationship between one man and one woman. This is the religious as well as the social idea that is behind the conception. Such was its Christian origin, to be sure, and in theological mandate and legal statute the spirit of this conception was written. Even to this day, divorce is denied by the Roman Catholic Church, and is sanctioned only under circumstances of a very extraordinary or extenuating character. The rise of divorce as a consideration in modern marital arrangements dates from the Reformation; as a practice, however, it does not become a factor until the nineteenth century. Divorce among the Romans falls within a different category. As is to be expected, from the economic alignments of society, divorce, even to this day in England, is practically forbidden to the poor by the sheer costliness of its procedure.[1] Only with the aristocratic classes, did divorce seem at all a social evil. The rest of society, with the exception of an occasional Milton, remained comparatively unaffected.

When we speak of marriage today, and the marital institution, it must not be thought that we are speaking of marriage in terms of historical evolution. If we say that marriage has decayed, we do not mean that people do not still marry, or that they will not marry in the future. In speaking of the bankruptcy of marriage we mean the bankruptcy of modern marriage and the

[1] The cost is from £30 to £40 at the very lowest; often it is far more expensive.

moral foundations upon which it has been constructed. Even under a state of "free love," people may marry, but their marriages may signify nothing more binding than ephemeral affections and alliances of a fortnight. Primitive marriage was marriage also, but with divorce as simple as marriage, it was based upon nothing other than the theory of free contract.[2] This theory of free contract is all that the modern revolutionist or free-lover desires. But this attitude is a violation, in fact is the very antithesis, of the *binding-contract* upon which modern marriage has been founded. It is marriage as we know it, therefore, the marriage of modern monogamy, of the binding-contract variety, our system of marriage, in other words, that has broken down, and today is bankrupt.

Divorce with primitive marriage was neither an important nor a disruptive factor. Nor was it with ancient marriage. With so-called primitive monogamy, for instance, we find that marital "relations exhibit all degrees of duration."[3] Divorce could be obtained by either sex by mutual consent.[4] In various other stages of primitive marriage, the woman had comparatively no rights at all, and the man could divorce her in ac-

[2] Encyclopaedia Britannica.
[3] Lichtenberger, "Divorce: A Study in Social Causation." University of Columbia Press.
[4] *Ibid.*

cordance with his whims. During the period of rape and wife-purchase, for example, the woman possessed no rights whatever. Of course, in the days of the mother-family, or matriarchate, the right of divorce rested entirely with the woman.[5] It was not until property interests arose as a significant element in social relations that marriage became conditioned by economic as well as sexual factors, and that entire freedom in divorce was at all restricted. It is only with the rise of private property, and the necessity of establishing legitimacy and inheritance, that the marital ceremony assumed a somewhat serious aspect. Even with this change, marriage remained a civil and not a religious act. With ancient peoples this attitude is at once obvious. Among the Jews, by way of illustration, marriage was an economic and not a religious contract. Polygamy was the approved relationship, and not monogamy. The husband had absolute authority in the matter of divorce. He did not even have to state a cause for divorcing his wife or wives; his decision was looked upon as a personal and not a social action.

"When a man taketh a wife and marrieth her, then it shall be, if she find favor in his eyes, because he hath found some unseemly thing in her, that he shall write her a bill of divorcement, and give it in her hand, and send her out

[5] Sumner, "Folkways."

[63]

of his house. And when she is departed out of his house, she may go and be another man's wife." [6]

With the Romans divorce at first had been relegated entirely to the husband, but with the later days of the Republic, *manus* marriage had been replaced by *free* marriage and in this latter stage marriage became a private affair, with divorce a private matter which the woman was as free to utilize as the man. No court or magistrate was needed to register or sanction the procedure. This was equivalent to a state of free love, as we mentioned before, with marriage existing side by side with it.

Christianity introduced a new attitude which has not yet been erased from the marital ceremony and institution. The concept of sex as a sin is intruded as an ethical attitude at this time, and the theory of indissoluble monogamy was forced upon the world. Divorce was destroyed. The words of Jesus: "What, therefore, God hath joined together, let not man put asunder," served as the cardinal doctrine for the Christian marriage. While Augustine had not denied the Biblical approval of polygamy, and the Pope had not frowned upon its existence, and indeed in the case of Henry IV of Castile had defended it, divorce was condemned by

[6] Quoted from Lichtenberger; *cf*. above.

both of them. While the Reformation achieved a change in this attitude, its character must not be misconstrued. For a time the sacramental aspect of marriage was subordinated to the civil. Luther in his own words had described marriage as "a worldly-transaction." Cromwell, in 1653 had had the civil marriage act passed. Men such as Milton, Zwingli, and Bullinger had argued in favor of the civil and against the religious concept of marriage. Nevertheless, this struggle was carried on more in opposition to the religious concept of marriage. Even to this day, for instance, despite the revolt of the Protestant sects marriage is still considered a sacred and divine institution.

The attitude toward marriage, thus, was not fundamentally altered. It is this foolish notion of marriage as something singularly sacred, or even divine, that handicapped the modern world in its attempts to change its arrangements and form. If civil marriage now became possible, it was not long accepted and practiced. Although the early Puritans in the United States, for instance, had a Huguenot clergyman indicted for solemnizing marriages in Boston, this revolt was not of long duration. Modern marriage, even in this advanced day, is usually performed within the precincts of religious jurisdiction. If the Reformation denied the doctrine of indissolubility and permitted the introduction of divorce, it did not destroy the idea of the sacred nature of marriage. Nor did it deny the inherent virtue of monogamy. In fact, it tightened the bonds of monogamy. This change, which is usually unemphasized and neglected, is of profound importance. While the Roman Catholic Church had been willing to concede the Biblical existence of polygamy, and, therefore, refrain from attack upon it as a practice—in fact even recommended it at times, as we have seen, the new churches and the new society condemned all polygamous relations as sinful. The cause of this change is not hard to trace. Protestantism had represented the rise of individualism, and the revolt of the middle classes against the feudal oppression of the Roman Catholic Church. The Roman Catholic Church was a feudal organization that adapted itself to the new economic order only with extreme difficulty and after painful compromise. Protestantism, springing up afresh and anew, was able to embody within its creeds the desires and demands of this commercial class.[7] To be more precise, Protestantism was an expression, a result of the rise, of this new economic group. This new economic group, which was constituted largely of the

[7] Preserved Smith, "The Reformation." Also see the author's book "Sex Expression in Literature," Chapter II.

trading class, and in England became known as the Puritans, depended upon commerce rather than land for its sustenance. Private property became more important with them than it had been with the landed groups in the age that had preceded. Their whole morality revolved about the concept of property-relations and property-contract.[8] Monogamy was indispensable to their economic life. The close-knit, unified monogamous family became an integral part of their existence. Puritan doctrine classified "money-making" as the most "God-given" of occupations. Their preachers maintained that any man who did not attempt to derive the utmost pecuniary profit from his enterprise failed to be "God's Steward." A man's success in business, in the words of preacher Steele, meant that "God had blessed his trade." Production was undertaken for profits in this new age of industrialism, and not for consumption, as had been characteristic of feudalism. It was this new economic attitude that was the driving power in the enforcement of this rigid morality of the bourgeoisie.

It was this economic attitude that necessitated the strict monogamy upon which the institution of modern marriage is erected. Despite the indissolubility of the marital tie, the attitude of the middle ages had been

[8] Rivers, "Social Organization."

[67]

much more lenient and flexible. Polygamy, as we saw, in places was permitted. Sex relations were often loose, and infidelities were more readily condoned. The revolt of woman in the twelfth century, for instance, would have been impossible in the seventeenth, eighteenth or nineteenth centuries. With the rise of the Protestant sects, and the era of commercialism and industrialism which swept us into our new world, we find, as Taine expressed it, "the eulogy of the family-tree, of domestic sweets, of orderly piety, and of home." Monogamous marriage, therefore, became more important than it had ever been during the earlier centuries of the Christian era. It was as a principle rather than a practice that divorce was discussed. As proof of this fact, we find that England did not actually change its theory of law in reference to divorce until the middle of the nineteenth century. Until 1858, the theory that prevailed was the same as that of the Roman Catholic Church.[9] The polemics of Milton never gained legislative consideration or endorsement. In instances of adultery and cruelty, nominal divorces were permitted, but in reality the marriages were not dissolved at all. The parties were instructed to separate, but they were not allowed to remarry. It was not until 1857 that a divorce court was established;

[9] Encyclopaedia Britannica.

and then it was only in the event of the wife's, not the husband's adultery that a divorce was granted.

Cromwell's interest in making marriage a civil instead of an ecclesiastical procedure was an evidence of his determination to prevent the control of the state by the church, and was an illustration of the influence of Luther and not of Calvin. In this action, however, he did not for a moment have in mind the idea of robbing marriage of its continuity. In truth, the bourgeoisie was interested, as we have shown, in making the marriage tie into a binding economic-contract, and the family into a orderly, harmonious unit. These things could only be realized through the institution of strict, monogamous marriage. Divorce would impair this institution. Frequent divorce would destroy it. That is why, despite discussion of the topic, it was not until 1857, as we described, that a divorce court was established in England.

A monogamy which is interrupted by frequent divorce is a monogamy only in fiction, but not in fact. The essential idea of monogamy, as we said, is a relationship of life-long duration. Otherwise Mr. Mencken's witticism: "Certainly I believe in monogamy, one woman at a time," is sound doctrine. In other words, if merely living with one woman at a time is monogamy, then many forms of free-love are fundamentally monogamous. Many an individual, then, classified by conventional society as a profligate or demirep, is genuine monogamist. But everyone knows that it is not in such ways that monogamy is construed. Monogamy is not a trial-and-error institution; many trials are condemned as much as many errors. Divorce in itself is a violation of the concept. Numerous divorces render it absurd. Bishop Charles Fiske, therefore, is not exaggerating when he describes the present trend in marriage as "a tide of consecutive polygamy."[10] And he is equally correct when he maintains that if you "take away the thought of finality and determination from the marriage vow" you rob it of its virtue and meaning.[11] It is in a state of decline and bankruptcy.

If the state of marriage in our society today is not one of "consecutive polygamy" it certainly is a monogamy that has become so modified that it is almost meaningless, except in the preservation of those property-rights which were originally inherent in its concept. Many find solace in this last reality. Many affirm the preference of a modified monogamy to an unmodified. But when these modifications become

[10] "Marriage, Temporary or Permanent." *Atlantic Monthly,* Volume 1 July-Dec. 1926.
[11] *Ibid.*

more numerous with each generation, the old idea of monogamy is soon converted into a myth. The end of these modifications, as we find in Soviet Russia today, is the complete annihilation of monogamy as a binding concept. Soviet Russia accepts monogamy too, but modified to such a point, as we shall see later, that freedom of divorce has made variation of wives easily attainable. "Consecutive polygamy" perhaps is as apt and accurate a description of the new relations as "modified monogamy." "Modified monogamy," it is true, is less offensive to the conservative conscience, permits a wider freedom, and, being less exposed to criticism, is, therefore, preferred by the multitude.

Let us observe some of the developments in divorce, which have effected this "consecutive polygamy" that has taken place in our modern world. In Holland there is now a divorce rate of fourteen for every one thousand marriages. In Sweden, there were seven divorces per thousand in 1899, 84 per thousand in 1904, and 97 per thousand in 1909. In Denmark divorces have increased from 550 to 650 out of a total of only 850,000 married persons. In the United States the figures are even more of a revelation. In 1880 the United States had thirty-eight divorces per hundred thousand of the population, and in 1900 it had 73 per hundred thousand. This increase was so startling and appalling that it attracted the attention of the world. Only Japan with an average of 215 per hundred thousand surpassed the American record. Between 1867 and 1886 there were 328,716 divorces, while between 1887 and 1906 there were 945,625. The following comparisons will illustrate the extensity of this increase:

	Population in the United States	Increase in the population	Increase in divorce per 100,000
1870	38,600,000	...	..
1880	50,000,000	79.4	39
1890	63,000,000	70.2	53
1900	76,000,000	67.6	73

The increase of divorces between 1870 and 1880 was two-and-two-thirds times greater than that of the increase in the population; between 1890 and 1900 it rose to three times.

In 1924, for instance, this number had risen to 151.

An effective comparison is to be seen in the statistics as to domestic relations in 1887 and 1924. In 1887 there was one divorce to every 17.3 marriages; in 1924 there was one divorce to every 6.9 marriages.

Here is another chart that shows the increase of divorce over every five preceding years, with the percentage increase over the five preceding years noted. The increase is about 30% for every five years, with the exception of 1892-96 when the economic depriva-

TABLE SHOWING INCREASE IN DIVORCE

Period of Years	Total Number	Increase over 5 Preceding Years	
1867–1871	53,574	. . . . .	. . . . .
1872–1876	68,547	14,973	27.9%
1877–1881	89,284	20,737	30.3%
1882–1886	117,311	28,027	31.4%
1887–1891	157,324	40,013	34.1%
1892–1896	194,939	37,615	23.9%
1897–1901	260,720	65,781	33.7%
1902–1906	332,642	71,922	27.6%

tions of the panic effected a decline in divorce as well as marriage.

"There were in 1924," writes Professor William Fielding Ogburn, "about 15 to 16 times as many divorces as there were in 1870, and yet the population is only about three times as large." [12]

In specific states, for instance, the conditions are even more astonishing. In Oregon, as we pointed out

[12] "Eleven Questions Concerning American Marriage"—*Social Forces,* Sept., 1927.

before, there is one divorce for every 2.6 marriages; in Wyoming one divorce for every 3.9 marriages; and in California one divorce for every 5.1 marriages. If we study divorce libels the conditions are even more astonishing. Divorce libels in Boston, for example, (or in Suffolk County) have increased almost three times as fast as marriages during the twenty years from 1900-1920.

In connection with these figures Arthur Garfield Hayes made an illuminating comment:

"Whatever effects it may have on society, the extension of grounds for divorce which has taken place in the last decade, and the modern improvement in communication and travel, which opens other states or foreign countries to an increasing number, *brings about a situation by which people, though not free to contract, do avail themselves of means which have the same effect.* Revolutionary changes occur unnoticed, while our delusions persist and our sense of conservatism is gratified." [13]

In other words, what Hayes has declared is that if people are not legally free to contract as they wish in their sexual relations, which would be equivalent to a form of free-love, they modify the law in such ways as to get this effect without being aware of it. They turn monogamy into such a malleable thing that

[13] "Modern Marriage and Ancient Law"—Arthur Garfield Hays.

it is no longer monogamy but a chaos of voluntary changes, rejections, and novelties, and yet in still calling it monogamy their fear of convention is pacified. They convert marriage into a kind of experimental liaison, with legal trappings to sanctify it, and convince themselves that by still calling it marriage the institution remains unassailed.

It is instructive also to observe the causes that are assigned for divorces. For example, among 945,625 divorces effected, 642,476 were granted to women, and 316,149 to men. Over two divorces, then, were granted to wives for every one that was granted to husbands, which signifies, in statistical form, an attitude on the part of woman that is distantly removed from that of her Victorian predecessors. In the nineteenth century divorce sought by woman was a sign of stigma. Women then were not to "take arms against a sea of trouble," but to accept it with resignation. Such response was supposed to be part of the innate nobility of her nature. Today woman is in a state of protest and revolt. At one time the double-morality was accepted as a phase of the inevitable. Today, as we know, it is denied. In the matter of desertion, we see a similar situation. Among 367,502 divorces granted on the basis of desertion, 211,219 were given to women, and 156,283 to men. This change is directly connected, of course, with the economic independence of woman that has become so marked in the present generation and which has so decisively influenced the new feminine psychology. Secondly, the overwhelming preponderance of desertion as the main cause of divorce is a revealing development. It is not that the popularity of desertion as a means of escaping an unhappy marriage is surprising, but the fact that desertion is found to be characteristic of the lower classes. While, at one time, as we indicated, divorce was entirely an upper-class privilege, and remains so even until now in England, we know that in America today all classes endeavor to utilize the opportunity it affords. The fact remains, nevertheless, that the poor, who are certainly not more happy than the prosperous, cannot afford to take advantage of the freedom of divorce with anything like the frequency that it can be taken advantage of by the rich. The poor man, therefore, has turned to desertion as his solution. "Desertion is the poor man's divorce" is a common saying among those confronted with the domestic problems of the proletariat.[14] Desertion is simple and economical.

Even the presence of children does not lessen desertions. For example, Miss Brandt, who investigated

[14] "Family Disorganization"—Ernest R. Mowrer—University of Chicago Press. 1927.

574 instances of desertion, discovered that only in 3.48% of the cases were there no children. In other words, the presence of children in these 96.52% cases was but an additional economic burden that made desertion an attractive escape. In the tendency to divorce, the presence of children, however, is a retarding factor. Divorce statistics reveal a striking absence of children on the part of those seeking to be divorced. This is because the presence of children in the middle and upper classes is not an incentive to separation, since the economic burden is not so acute or oppressive. To be certain, a score of other factors are involved, in many cases, and this explanation, as a consequence, can only be noted as descriptive of a tendency to which there are bound to be exceptions.

In America the grounds for divorce vary with almost every state in the union. The chaos is extremely annoying and troublesome. It is almost as bad as certain of the marital laws that exist in different states. One white man, for instance, who had married a colored woman in Chicago, where intermarriage between white and colored people is legal, found that when he moved to Maryland he would be imprisoned if he lived with his wife. When he insisted upon his natural rights as a husband he was informed that he could not even get a divorce since in the eyes of Maryland he had never been married. Such cases are numerous. In Reno one can get a divorce after a residence of three months, on the ground of cruelty or one year's desertion. In New York one can get a divorce only on the grounds of adultery, or proof of the unchastity of a wife before marriage. At the same time New York permits a common law marriage. In one case there was a man who was a bigamist in one state and a monogamist in another. There are other instances in which children can be legitimate in one state and illegitimate in another. South Carolina, curiously enough, permits no divorce at all. Nevertheless, its compensations are in other directions. *It does not make adultery an indictable offense, and it has actually passed a law, regulating the amount of property, a man can bestow upon his concubine.*[15] This is one of the most unique gestures of compromise on record. Rather than modify its marital code, and concede the existence of necessary difficulties and deviations in marital relationships, it invents another law to circumscribe these deviations without violating the original statute. Thus the old seems firm and unchanged, although in reality it has been fundamentally altered.[16]

[15] "Marriage and Divorce"—Johnson.

[16] If statistics mirror correctly the expression of attitudes, then certainly the looseness or rigidity of divorce laws does not multiply the desire for domestic separations. At least, liberal divorce laws do

Divorce has menaced the marital institution in every country in Europe as well as America. In Germany divorces rose from 13,344 in 1918 to 36,542 in 1920; in Switzerland from 1,699 in 1918 to 2,241 in 1920; in Sweden from 1,098 in 1918 to 1,455 in 1923. In the United States, with 180,868 actual divorces (an advance of 3.1% over the 1925 record) and 3,823 annulments in the year 1926, it is apparent, the increase has been the most widespread and profound. This condition has produced an amusing farce. In order to protect the family and solidify the marital couple, suggestions and reforms have been legion. One county in West Virginia gives a cook-book with each marriage license; the United States Department of Commerce issues a pamphlet "How to Own Your

not necessitate frequent divorces, nor astringent divorce laws effect infrequency of divorces. If people wish to separate, there are inevitable ways of "getting around the law." This is proven by the example of the United States. In the United States where divorce laws are certainly not characterized by any marked flexibility or laxness, there is one divorce for approximately every six marriages. In England, also, where the old divorce laws are only slightly modified, divorces have been increasing with every year. In France, on the contrary, where everything has been done to make it more difficult to marry but less difficult to divorce—where divorce is considered "neat, quick, and secret"—there is only one divorce in five marriages. From 1918 and 1919, for instance, the number of divorces in France rose from 7,851 to 11,514; but in England with its far stricter divorce laws, the numbers rose from 2,222 in 1918 to 7,044 in 1921.

Home," and asserts that the ownership of one's home is at the basis of marital felicity. The *Pictorial Review,* which essays to protect the old morality and at the same time its purse-strings, features a special brief:

HOW TO BE HAPPY THOUGH MARRIED

In the past seven years Chief Justice Joseph Sabath, of Chicago, has disposed of no fewer than 25,000 divorce cases, which should at least qualify him to express an opinion on the subject of marital happiness. In a recent interview the eminent jurist advised all husbands and wives to follow these rules in order to be reasonably contented:

Bear and forbear.

Work together, play together, and grow up together.

Avoid heated quarrels.

Do not cover up little differences until they accumulate.

Speak out frankly to each other until you reach an agreement.

Sympathy, good humor, and mutual understanding are the supporting pillars of the home.

Good humor on parting in the morning and a cheerful meeting in the evening.

Share all responsibilities and pleasures alike.

By all means, establish a home of your own, regardless of how humble it may be.

Make your bedtime prayers a sort of review of the day, and you will never go to bed without a "clean slate" and there will be no "leftovers" for next morning.

The wife should realize that she has built her house upon shifting sands, and should set to work to build a sure foundation. She must show her husband that she loves him; that thoughts of other men are beneath her; that he insults her by his suspicion.

The husband should make his wife a real partner, discuss his problems with her, show her that he actually loves her, supply her with enough funds to run the home, be faithful and not commit indiscretions that will lay him open to suspicion of graver things.

2.

The "hostility felt today toward the marriage order," [17] which Count Keyserling laments, is to be found in active expression in the literature of our era. The current attitude toward marriage has reverted to attack in the form of satire and ridicule. In passing it is arresting to observe that there is a pronounced similarity between the attitude toward marriage which prevailed during the seventeenth century in Restoration England, when the marital system had undergone a sharp downfall among the upper classes, and the one that is manifest today. The remarks of the Restorationists often seem almost modern in character. Heartwell's ejaculation, in Congreve's play, *The Old Batchelour,*

[17] "The Book of Marriage"; Count Keyserling.

"Marry you? No, no, I'll love you,"

sounds as familiar as a Shavian epigram.

"Away, in the old days people married where they loved; but that fashion is changed, child."

"Every man plays the fool once in his life; but to marry is playing the fool all one's life long."

Congreve's wit has a contemporaneity that is uncanny. The satire of Wycherly, Vanbrugh, and Sedley was scarcely less penetrating and piquant.

"Get money enough," says Bellamira in Sir Charles Sedley's play, *The Eunuch*, "and you can never want a husband. A husband is a good bit to close one's stomach with, when love's feast is over. Who would begin a meal with cheese?"

Here Wycherly through the mouth of Horner:

"Let me tell you, women, as you say, are like soldiers, made constant and loyal by good pay, rather than by oaths and covenants, therefore I'd advise my friends to keep rather than to marry."

If contemporary literature is not as scintillating in its satire, or as clever in its attack, it is not because its sentiment is alien to this outlook. The contempt for "middle-class morality" that rides upon almost every witticism in *Pygmalion* is akin to the mockery and sarcasm of these early Comedy writers. Shaw, to be sure, has been only one of the leaders in this modern assault upon bourgeois marriage. Ibsen, Brieux, Galsworthy, W. L. George, Hardy, Joyce, Wassermann, Pretzang, Werfel, Yessenin, Dreiser, Anderson, Cocteau, Morand, Barbusse, D'Annunzio, Wells, are but a few random figures who at one time or another have plunged into the attack.

In Somerset Maugham's play, *A Constant Wife,* the old morality and the old marriage make a merry funeral. In *Saturday's Children* Maxwell Anderson intrudes the same conflict. The father in the play is created in order to reflect the influence of the new upon the old. The father who learned to "swear" from his daughters, is a conspicuous contrast to the mother who is always bewailing the fact that "it was all so different then." The father, modernized by experience, advises his daughter, who has already been initiated into the pathos and ennui of marital existence, that she should not have married, because all marriage is tragic folly.

"Marriage is no love affair, my dear. It's little old last year's love affair. It's a house and bills and dishpans and family quarrels. That's the way the system beats you. They bait the wedding with a romance and they hang a three-hundred-pound landlord around your neck and drown you in grocery bills. If I'd talked to you that night I'd have said—if you're in love with him, why, have your affair, sow a few oats. Why the devil should the boys have a monopoly on wild oats?"

Then he advises her:

"Fall in love—have your affair—and when it's over—get out!"

In "The World of William Clissold," Wells flays the marital institution, and comments with enthusiasm upon its fading influence.

"But a good number of people believe in marriage these days," says the housekeeper in Gustav Wied's play, $2 \times 2 = 5$.

"Yes," replied the protagonist, "but a good number believe in Santa Claus."

In *The Doctor's Dilemma*, we have one of George Bernard Shaw's characters declare:

"I don't believe in morality. . . . Morality consists in being suspicious of other peoples' not being legally married."

As one revolutionary critic stated, these quick-fire shots into the substance of middle-class morality have made even the middle-class appreciate the nature of their own stupidities and foolish conventions. Even the middle-class thus came to laugh at middle-class marriage. The inspiration of their morality, through satire and ridicule, thus became the laughing-stock of its own class—at least its upper set.

In consonance with the same spirit, Johan Van
Vorden, a new Dutch novelist, in his recent novel
"Alex Vrouwen" ("Alexander's Women"), has one of
his female characters assert:

"If a woman who is free does not want to bind a man
legally to herself—not even when she imagines she is justified to do so—but allows him to be her lover, this means
the greatest honor a woman can bestow on a man. Never
in her life could she give a greater proof of love and respect
at the same time."

In *The Fanatics,* Miles Malleson assails the old morality, with its idiotic and absurd asceticisms, and re-
serves only scorn for the old concept of marriage.

Such citation of contemporary literature that attacks
or satirizes marriage as an institution we could continue indefinitely if further evidence were needed. The
sentiment is so obvious and keenly felt in almost every
literary effort concerned with modern life that additional illustrations would only prove irksomely repe-
titious.

The vociferous regrets and admonitions of the clergy
have already become familiar utterance. Journalists,
psychologists, philosophers, lawyers, judges, and physicians have reiterated the same cry. One preacher

urges that unhappy couples remain together, arming themselves with the fortitude of resignation, so that the family may be saved from ruin. Another furnishes a new ethical recipe for the salvation of the marital couple. Bishop Manning denounces divorce as our greatest social evil, and in bitter, scathing, and sensational style deprecates the endeavors of those who would reform marriage by modifying certain of its aspects. Declaring that divorce "breaks down the sanctity of marriage", he directed an important angle of his attack upon "a group in the Church itself which had suggested consideration of unmarried unions with the use of birth-control to guard against the coming of children. In this particular diatribe against the new attitude and ideals, he gave vivid indication of the changing sentiment toward marriage which is no longer secretive in expression. Even the Church has been affected. Even a few ecclesiastics are willing to adjust their ethics to the new environment. The Reverend Dr. Caleb R. Stetson, rector of Trinity Episcopal Church, for instance, maintains that:

"It is conceivable that this government might some day make polygamy legal . . . (and) that legalized polygamy has certain features which recommend it, *as compared with the progressive polygamy and respectable promiscuity toward which we are now tending.*" (Italics mine.)

Rev. Dr. Stetson has stated his opinions with singular candor in the "Year Book of Trinity Parish." In another place he adds:

"There is a definite propaganda for a freer divorce . . . which may even come to a point where trial marriages may be legalized, or to the condition in Soviet Russia where divorce is granted without question on the application of both or even of one of the parties to a marriage."

These statements of the Rector are an excellent index to the nature of the times. After all, the Rev. Stetson is not a radical ecclesiastic; he is not a Bishop Brown, dedicating his energy to the cause of the proletariat, nor even a Stickney Grant, challenging outworn medievalisms in the name of truth. He is simply a clergyman who realizes the world has changed, and that marriage has changed with the world. The Rev. Stetson is not the only clergyman who is cognizant of the catastrophic changes which have undermined the marital institution . The clergy, as a whole, appreciates and deplores it. Jeremiads against the laxity of modern marriage resound from multitudes of pulpits.

It is not surprizing, then, that Professor John B. Watson's prognostication that:

"the present marriage system will end in fifty years . . . that (since) the mystery of marriage has been broken down

[87]

. . . we must have a new kind of ethic, based on a scientific study of human behavior as a way to more simple marital adjustments"

did not disturb nor terrify the public. Such predictions are no longer uncommon. A century ago, or even two generations ago, however, such a declaration would have aroused horror and disdain. Such utterances, then, were considered the attributes of lunacy and far-flung fanaticism. A few radicals might entertain and cherish such notions, but these radicals scarcely constituted a fragmentary fringe of the public opinion which prevailed. They were social pariahs, and their ideas isolated dogmas that touched the imagination only of the maniac. In the last generation the change has occurred. We have been rushed and plunged across so many new horizons and twisting seas that the very tempo of our life has been broken and changed, and its rhythm shaken into somersaulting jerk and recoil.

The bankruptcy of marriage is closely bound up with all of the changes we have previously recorded, the moral shell-shock of the World War, the chaos of the new morality, the decline of ethical idealism among the upper classes, but particularly with the rising economic independence of the modern woman. Its main basis is to be found, as Beatrice Hinkle contends, in "the dislodgment of marriage from the supreme place in the interest and life of women." The new woman has new interests, new attractions, new ideals.

CHAPTER V

THE NEW MORALITY IN AMERICA

WITH the breakdown of the old morality, and the decay of modern marriage, which have grown out of the conditions of contemporary life, a new morality has been the inevitable consequence of the chaos. This new morality in America as yet has evolved no criteria of conduct that are definite or decisive. It is still embryonic in form. It flutters about for a freedom that it fears to admit as other than a secret aspiration. Although it has had widespread social expression, it, unhappily, still remains a revolt of individuals rather than of groups. The individual equation continues paramount. While greater liberty has been attained, it has been through the adventurous intelligence of individual initiative and not the advancing wisdom of social progress. As a result, while the sweep of protest on the part of youth has become social in its manifestations, the revolt of the individual is forced to be clandestine rather than courageous. On the whole, it is neither sincere nor candid, neither straightforward nor honest. If it is no longer timid, it is still evasive.

While men have always been known to sow their "wild oats" before marriage, the moral concept of prenuptial chastity denied this privilege to women. With the revolt of youth, however, and the emancipating enthusiasms of the new morality, this condition has changed. The "sowing of wild oats" is no longer the particular prerogative of the man.

As Alyse Gregory wrote, in discussing the "New Morality of Women":

"However unwilling one may be to acknowledge it, girls begin to sow their wild oats. . . . Girls, from well-bred, respectable middle-class families (have) broken through those invisible chains of custom and asserted their right to a nonchalant, self-sustaining life of their own with a cigarette after every meal and a lover in the evening to wander about with and lend color to life. If the relationship (becomes) more intimate than such relationships are supposed to be, there (is) nothing to be lost that a girl could not well dispense with. Her employer asks no question as to her life outside the office. She (has) her own salary at the end of the month, and (asks) no other recompense from her lover but his love and companionship." [1]

[1] "The Changing Morality of Women." *Current History*, November, 1923.

It is not only that girls are beginning to sow their
wild oats, however, that is important, but that they
are usually forced to conceal it from their elders by
device and subterfuge that lead to personal detriment
and harm. Certain forms of sexual expression, nevertheless, that once were forbidden, have now become
customary instead of exceptional. Kissing, for example, which once was supposed to begin only with
the gesture of betrothal, has now become a promiscuous pastime. "Necking" has become an accepted practice. The modern dance, of course, has stimulated
these open liberties in conduct. *The automobile has
given to them the convenience of expression that the
fire-side parlor, with parents vigilant behind door or
curtain, would never have permitted.*[2] So widespread
has been the growth of these phenomena, that a demand that "necking" be made esthetic has become
urgent. *The New Student,* the most liberal and intelligent of American student publications, suggests, for instance, the creation of an All-University Necking
Parlor:

"Yet, although necking is a highly pro-moral activity

[2] The exceptional importance of the automobile as a factor in
the development of the new morality can scarcely be exaggerated.
It has provided an easy means of escape that hitherto had been very
difficult and thus enabled revolt to convert itself from verbal to
active forms.

and hence should be fostered, certain refinements are needed in its technique. Moralizing and legislation have placed the stigma—and hence the attraction—primarily on the physical, i.e., tactual, aspect of petting parties. Their æsthetic and artistic possibilities have consequently been left unnoticed. . . .

"Love, as even preachers have been fond of telling us, has been the cause of the greatest artistic inspiration down the ages. But not in Puritanical communities—where, indeed, there has been no great art. . . . They marry, of course, they produce children, they propagate the race; but I would venture to say, they do not love, as Europeans have loved; they do not exploit the emotion, analyze and enjoy it, still less express it in manners, in gesture, in epigram, in verse.

"Now, petting parties represent the crude, inchoate beginnings made by American youth to break away from this prevalent conception of eroticism as merely a mechanism of propagation, or as a brute, delightful sin. Some delicate-spirited boys and girls have already developed necking into a fine art.

"The art, however, at present has its limitations. Necking must be done furtively in the back seat of a broken-down Ford, or in some uncomfortable cranny of a stone wall, and in the dark. And in the dark, as Jurgen remarks, 'almost anything is rather more than likely to happen.' These, to say the least, are not conditions favorable to the punishment of any art.

"What we need, obviously, is an All-University Necking Parlor, a sort of temple of Venus or Garden of Ashtaroth, in which the amatory arts could be cultivated under æsthetic influence. . . .

"In this Garden of Ashtaroth—the amorosities could be conducted to the ethereally sensuous strains of Beethoven, Chopin, and Strauss. The sofas—or, at first, to give a more familiar atmosphere, the porch-swings—as well as the rest of the furnishings of the place, should be of artistic design, and on the walls should be reproductions of famous love-paintings by Botticelli, Turner and Correggio. On the tables should be books of verse by only the great love poets such as Swinburne, Rossetti, Petrarch, Gautier, Heine, Sidney and Spenser. The effect of this, too, should be beneficial, as at present the ditties in *Hot Dog* and *Whiz Bang* are the only verses quoted between sexes." [3]

If this suggestion seems to smack somewhat of the ridiculous, it does not the less, therefore, fail in its attempt to depict the tendency in the now morals. Certain forms of behavior have become so common that they no longer evoke astonishment or reprehension. "Necking" which once, not many years ago, would have been attacked as an indecent perversion, and a violation of every canon of moral conduct, is now accepted as a natural phenomenon.

[3] *The New Student.*

Like Eunice Hoyt in Upton Sinclair's novel "Oil," these youths accept the ideal of Bertrand Russell that "all sexual intercourse should spring from the free impulse of both parties, based upon mutual inclination, and nothing else." [4] And out of this revolt matures the woman who realizes that she is "far from what man has always asserted she was, timid, prudish and monogamous"; on the other hand she discovers that she "is bold, immodest, and polyandrous." [5]

The reasoning of Eunice Hoyt is fairly typical of modern youth:

"Driving back to Beach City they talked about this adventure. Bunny hadn't thought much about sex, he had no philosophy ready at hand, but Eunice had hers, and told it to him simply and frankly. The old people taught you a lot of rubbish about it, and then they sneaked off and lived differently, and why should you let yourself be fooled by silly 'don'ts'? Love was all right if you were decent about it, and when you had found out that you didn't have to have any babies, why must you bother to get married? Most married people were miserable anyhow, and if the young people could find a way to be happy, it was up to them, and what the old folks didn't know wouldn't hurt them.

[4] "Styles in Ethics"—*The Nation.* April 30, 1924.
[5] Woman's Morality in Transition," Dr. Joseph Collins. *Current History,* Oct. 1927.

"Did Bunny see anything wrong with that? Bunny answered that he didn't; the reason he had been such 'an old prude' was just that he hadn't got to know Eunice. She said that men were supposed not to care for a girl who made advances to them; therefore she added with her flash of mischief, it would be up to Bunny to make some of the advances from now on. . . .

"Were there other girls like Eunice, Bunny wanted to know, and she said there were plenty, and named a few, and Bunny was surprised and a little shocked, because some of them were prominent in class affairs, and decorous-seeming. Eunice told him about their ways, and it was a good deal like a secret society, without any officers or formal ritual, but with a strict code none the less. They called themselves the 'Zulus,' these bold spirits who had dared to do as they pleased; they kept one another's secrets faithfully, *and helped the younger ones to that knowledge which was so essential to happiness.* The old guarded this knowledge jealously—how to keep from having babies, and what to do if they got 'caught.' There was a secret lore about the art of love, and books that you bought in certain stores, or found stowed away behind other books in your father's den. Such volumes would be passed about and read by the scores.

"It was a new ethical code that these young people were making for themselves, without any help from their parents." (Italics mine.)[6]

[6] "Oil" by Upton Sinclair. Pages 196, 197.

Or the cry of Rachel in another section of the novel is not less indicative:

"I want to know that you love me, and that I'm free to love you. What do I care about preachers or justices?" [7]

While one scholar at Columbia University planned to send out five thousand questionnaires to both old and young people in an endeavor to definitely differentiate, by way of statistical average, the contrasting attitudes of the old and the new generation, and professors and students have used sundry methods of inquiry in order to glean facts and figures that would indicate the extensity of this revolution in human behavior, the one man in America who is best equipped to disclose the nature of this phenomenon is Judge Ben Lindsey. Lindsey was judge of the Juvenile Court in Denver for a period of twenty-six years. In this court he achieved one of the most unique experiments in America. He made this court into a laboratory for moral advice and instruction. His attitude was not that of a legalist, but a humanitarian. Youths came to him because they saw in him a friend and not a jurist. They confided in him because they trusted him. What they would have trembled to confess to their parents, they frankly told this sympathetic adviser. There was no camouflage about their confessions. It was un-

[7] *Ibid.*, Page 502.

necessary; indeed it was a hindrance. Candour in this court at least prevailed. While elsewhere youth had to live upon lies, here it could survive upon truth. Thousands and thousands of young men and women came to him in the course of years with their difficulties, predicaments and sufferings. What the teacher was unaware of, the minister insensitive to, and the parents unable to perceive, Judge Lindsey saw, heard, and understood. As a consequence, it is no exaggeration to say that he, above all others in America, is in a position to observe the change and trend of morals as expressed in the everyday life of modern youth. While his contacts may have been confined largely to the citizens of Denver, no one would be so ridiculous as to contend that the situation in Denver is an anomaly.

"The conditions I portray," wrote Ben Lindsey in his book, "The Revolt of Modern Youth," "are not peculiar to Denver. They hold even more true for every city and town in the United States."

In the introductory chapter of "The Revolt of Modern Youth" Judge Lindsey notes

"the growing signs of rebellion on the part of modern youth; a rebellion which is youth's instinctive reaction against a system of taboos, tribal superstitions, intolerances, and hypocrisies."

The revolt is not instinctive, of course, because things instinctive do not depend upon social change for their manifestation. If instinctive, then they were as instinctive in 1827 as in 1927. It is the changed environment, which we have described, that has created it.

Lindsey's picture of the attitude of these young people toward the problems of sex is revealed more vividly in his cases than in his conclusions. In the actual experiences of these youths, rather than in their words or the theories of those who would interpret them, is to be found the most convincing evidence of the trend of these new morals.

"I inquired (of her) more particularly. I learned that one could go automobile riding at fifteen, then one could drink freely when one was eighteen; that love making could begin at any time. Kissing, petting, and other tentative excursions into sex experience, provided they were not too pronounced, were taken for granted by this sweet-faced girl as part of what she might properly look forward to long before she was eighteen—if she could manage not to get found out. Such was her code, and such was the code of her friends and intimates.

"As to the question of actual sex experience, she hadn't yet come to definite conclusions, but she had an open mind. She debated this with me at length and with a candor based

[99]

on her knowledge that confidences imparted in my court are never betrayed. She inclined to the view that promiscuity in sex matters might be wrong, but that there was something to be said for the trial marriage or experimental liaisons, considering that most all the marriages she knew of seemed to be ending in divorce. She wondered if it was not more immoral for a man and woman to live together in marriage when they didn't love than it would be for another man and woman to live together, though unmarried, because they did love each other.

" 'Where do you get these ideas?' I asked. 'Where do you learn about such questions?'

" 'Oh, we girls talk about them; and some of the girls talk about these things with the boys; but I have never done that yet.' "

In this case we are confronted with the attitude of the young girl who is still torn with doubts, still unsettled of conclusions, but in revolt, nevertheless, against the traditions of her elders. Such cases are frequent. Here is another one with a somewhat different slant:

" 'Well, Mary,' I said when we were through with that, 'what about yourself?'

" 'Oh,' she said, carelessly, 'I'm going with Bill Riggs.'

" 'Is Bill your steady?'

" 'Sure,' she said; and then, without any reservations she

told me the whole story. It was considerably more scandalous than her interested relative had dreamed. She saw nothing wrong with it. She and Bill, she pointed out, had loved on the square like a true married pair, but this business of promiscuous petting that Maude was going in for was quite another matter. It was shocking. Maude must be made to——

" 'Well, Mary,' I put in, 'why don't you and Bill get married?'

" 'Married!' she said derisively. 'Why, Judge, out of ten girls in my set who have gotten married in the last two years more than half are divorced or separated from their husbands. Look at all that scandal. For instance, there was Jenny Strong. She testified in court that her husband didn't want her to have a baby, and made her go to an abortionist. None of that for me. If Bill and I don't get along, we'll quit without any fuss.'

" 'But what about babies?'

" 'I haven't thought about that yet much. I'm not sure I want any.'

" 'But suppose you do. That would be a different situation, wouldn't it?'

" 'Oh, no,' she said. 'Bill would marry me any time. He wants to. He's crazy about me. But I'm not sure I want to marry him. I haven't any too much confidence in Bill's capacity. Why, I'm earning more than he is right now.' "

We could multiply these cases into a myriad, perhaps, without exhausting Lindsey's material. Here is one girl who says that "at least fifty percent of those who begin with hugging and kissing do not restrict themselves to that," but "go the limit," and here is another who is ensnared in a "sex scrape" while her father, a minister, is crusading against vice. The cases are as multifarious in their diverse ramifications as they are similar in their general protest.

Lindsey, anxious to be conservative and not extreme, maintains that at least from fifteen to twenty-five percent of these girls unquestionably include the sexual act within the category of their relations with men. That this statement is guilty more of exaggeration in the cause of caution than that of fact is borne out by other revelations and conclusions in Lindsey's book. The assertions of youths themselves, when they attempt to estimate the extensity of the new freedom among the groups with which they are intimate, makes such a small estimate seem absurd. After all, Lindsey was confronted only with those cases that resulted in disaster or distress. The myriads of cases that did not terminate in difficulty or catastrophe, of course, never came to the knowledge of either Lindsey or the world. It is only fair to Lindsey to add, however, that he admits this fact, and in the following paragraphs, quoted from his book, "The Revolt of Modern Youth," he states that he has at hand certain figures which

"indicate with certainty that for every case of sex delinquency discovered, a very large number completely escape
detection. For instance, out of 495 girls at high-school age
—though not all of them were in high school—who admitted
to me that they had sex experiences with boys, only 25 became pregnant. That is about 5 percent, a ratio of one
in twenty. The others avoided pregnancy, some by luck,
others because they had a knowledge of more or less effective
contraceptive methods—a knowledge, by the way, which I
find to be more common among them than is generally
supposed.

"Now the point is this: First, that three-fourths of that
list of nearly five hundred girls came to me of their own
accord for one reason or another. Some were pregnant,
some were diseased, some were remorseful, some wanted
counsel, and so on. Second, the thing that always brought
them to me was their acute need for help of some kind.
Had they not felt that need, they would not have come.
For every girl who came for help, there must have been a
great many, a majority, who did not come because they
did not want help, and, therefore, kept their own counsel.

"In other words, that 500—covering a period of less than
two years—represented a small group, drawn from all levels
of society, that didn't know the ropes, and got into trouble
of one kind or another; but there was as certainly a much
larger group who did know the ropes, and never came
around at all. My own opinion is that for every girl who

comes to me for help because she is pregnant or diseased, or in need of comfort, there are many more who do not come because they escape scot free of consequences, or else because circumstances are such that they can meet the situation themselves. Hundreds, for instance, resort to the abortionist. I don't guess this, I know it."

In another place Lindsey is even more definite in his calculations:

"Consider, for example, that for every one of those 769 girls of high-school age whom I helped in the biennial period of 1920 and 1921, there was at least one other girl whom this court knew nothing about and never reached. That, surely, is as conservative an estimate as can be asked. And yet, conservative as it is, let us see where it leads. It involves a *minimum* of 1500 girls of high-school age (not necessarily in school) in Denver as having indulged in some kind of sex delinquency. It involves the assumption that 608 of them were actually in school. Assuming that there are about 3000 girls, then, attending the high schools of Denver, that figure 608 would represent about 20 percent over the period of two years, or 304 for each year, 10 percent per annum. It would mean that one high-school girl in every ten, or ten in every hundred in our high schools, have their feet set on more or less perilous paths, are subjecting themselves to regrettable risks, and are in need of guidance and, counsel for one reason or another.

"Let me repeat that these are minimum figures, and that

they include only the ages of 14, 15, 16 and 17. They do not include the ages 18, 19, 20 where there is doubtless a larger percentage of such delinquency. Let me remind the reader also of my conviction already stated, for every sexually delinquent girl we deal with there are an unknown number, possibly a much larger number, who escape our attention."

"Very good, we found from our own records that of 495 girls we dealt with who confessed to illicit sex relations only 1 in 20 encountered pregnancy. In that case, 100 pregnancies, taken care of by us, implies, on a ratio of 1 to 19, at least 1900 escapes from pregnancy; and 200 pregnancies would imply 3800 escapes from pregnancy. *And that among the girls of high-school age, some in school and some out of school, in a city of 300,000 population.* And these figures, let me say again, represent a *minimum* below the level of probability and common sense. The number of cases is certainly very far above what even these figures indicate."

We have quoted so abundantly from Lindsey because it is in his work that we can come so close to human materials. He has been more intimate with youth than have social workers or Sunday-school reformers.[8] He has been able to compute averages from a comparative enormity of statistics. If his analysis of his findings may verge, at times, upon the senti-

[8] What does the younger generation think about Judge Lindsey's book "Companionate Marriage?" Here are some opinions expressed

mental, if his sociological illations are shopworn and stodgy, if his suggestions and solutions are often impractical and inadequate, his facts are free of these limitations. He has collected his evidence with a studious sincerity. His honesty is impeccable; his courage is of that rare and excellent quality seldom seen in this age. What he may lack in sociological penetration he makes up for in humanitarian sympathy.

Much of the other work in America that has touched upon this problem of the revolt of youth and the growth of the new morality, is lacking in factual substance as compared with the work of Lindsey. There have been numerous studies of sexual delinquency, which often have been hopelessly evasive and incomplete. They have frequently been made by those

by undergraduate commentators in college and university journals. "Why has such a hurricane been raised by this book?" asks *The Dartmouth.* "More power to the Judge! He has stimulated some much needed discussion." "What his whole argument amounts to is a plea for a frank recognition of social custom already in force," declares *The Varsity,* of Columbia University. "The younger generation will read his book most understandingly." "This is a book that will sure shock our fathers," comments the *Red and Blue* (University of Penna.) "But if you are of the modern youth, who see life as it really is, you will see the wisdom of his words." "He has brought to bear on modern marriage a mind that sees through the illogical, stupid rules and conventions of society . . . and gives a practical solution to the problem," according to *The Daily Northwestern,* and *The Critical Review* of New York University calls him "America's most courageous standard-bearer of real, honest to goodness morality."

anxious to prove the strength of the old traditions.
Lindsey has correctly categorized "these unfortunate
zealots (who) busy themselves to such an extent with
surveys and graphs and mathematical computations,
(that) they clean forget that they have to do with
people. Most of it is fit only for Ph.D. theses, with
footnotes and book references at the bottom of each
page."

Material of interest in connection with the problem
of the new morality has been gathered by Katharine
Bement Davis. Dr. Davis has often been cited by
editorial writers as an opponent of Lindsey, and her
statistics grossly exaggerated by them in an endeavor
to prove that the old morals are unshaken. Certain
of the questions asked in her questionnaires, from time
to time, we shall find of exceptional interest and importance. Among the 1,000 women included in the
study of one questionnaire only 375 are cited as having allowed "spooning with their fianceé before marriage; [9] 208 allowed themselves to be kissed; and 389
allowed no liberties at all. Only seventy-one of these
women had had sexual intercourse prior to marriage.

[9] It is of no little amusement and interest to note the change in
terminology from "spooning" in the early days, to "necking," in these
modern days. The difference in expression of the two words alone,
is revealing of a sharp alteration of attitude. "Spooning" has about

Thirty-five of them had sex relations only with their fianceé, twelve had intercourse with one person only, sixteen with more than one person, and eight did not specify the person involved. Of the sixteen who had had intercourse with more than one person, ten posssessed information as to contraceptive technique, two had no information, and one did not reply at all.[10] Of these sixteen, six were college graduates, one a Master of Arts and one an M.D. Two had several years of college education; three were high school graduates, three had one or two years in high school, one had only advanced to the eighth grade, and one had had private tutoring.

The great number of these women who only allowed themselves to be kissed previous to marriage, and the greater number who did not allow any caress at all, might seem to indicate a conventionality of behavior on the part of women that would deny the triumph of the flapper and the rise of the new morality. An examination of these women, from the point of view of age, however, does not confirm this conclusion. The majority of them were in their thirties and forties when they answered this questionnaire in 1921 and

it that Victorian sweetness of disguise, "necking" has the modern roughness and candour of expression.

[10] "Sex Life of the Normal Married Woman"—*Journal of Social Hygiene*—Jan., 1923.

1922, and, therefore, do not represent the new generation which has become conspicuous by revolt. They
represent the generation that immediately preceded.
Even this generation, it is apparent, nevertheless, did
not represent in very perfect manner the closed-in
morals of their Victorian ancestors. In the matter of
abortions, for instance, we find that 93 of these 1000
women had abortions, one of them having had as many
as eight and nineteen of them having had two. And
while only seventy-one had sexual intercourse before
marriage, one hundred and sixty-three of them had
homosexual relations in the physical expression, and
381 had practiced masturbation. In many other ways
also, different and more subtle questions would have
shown that if these women do not represent the modern
generation, there was to be found, even in their attitude,
an emphatic sign of the revolt that has burst upon us
with the youth of today.

If we turn to a questionnaire that was privately
distributed at Amherst, the results disclosed will immediately be seen to sustain our previous contentions.
This questionnaire is even more limited in its numerical
scope than that of Dr. Davis, but far less timid and
evasive in its approach and far more direct in its inquiries. This questionnaire was called a questionnaire
on morals. The idea originally arose in the reference

to the absence of purity among the college men in America today. Only twenty-six cases were included in the inquiry, but the fact that the answers were solicited in open, oral fashion, with a group supervising in order to conduct the entire project in a careful, critical manner, gives the results a value that is unusual for such a small category of cases. In some instances men objected to answering the questions openly, but admitted a willingness to do so in private; wherever there was any doubt as to the authenticity of the answer, or the presence of any obscurity in reply, the answer was rejected and the vote discounted. The results, therefore, are as close an approach to accuracy as a questionnaire method of this kind could attain.

Here is a chart of the answers to eight of the questions:

QUESTIONNAIRE AND ANSWERS

	Yes	*No*
1. (*a*) Have you ever "necked"?	26	o
(*b*) Have you ever "necked" five or more women?	24	2
2. Have you ever "petted"?	23	3
3. (*a*) Have you ever drunk (1) Gin? (2) Scotch? (3) Rye? (4) Beer? (5) Wine?	17*	o

(*b*) Have you ever drunk a quart in an evening (Not beer and wine)...	12	7
4. Have you ever visited a house of ill fame?.	6	20
5. (*a*) Have you ever copulated?	7	19
(*b*) With more than five women?	5	21
(*c*) Ever more than three times in one night?	2	24
6. (*a*) Have you ever committed adultery?.	3	23
(*b*) Have you ever masturbated more than twice a week?	15	11

* (1)3; (2)4; (3)5; (4)4.

Now there are several conclusions of importance that are at once suggested by these answers. In the first place, it should be remembered, according to the statement of Mr. Walter C. Hughes, who was chiefly instrumental in the projection of this questionnaire, that these twenty-six students are assuredly representative of the average student in the university if not of those who are a "little purer" than the average. In brief, it was not a selected group chosen in order to illustrate a preconceived theory or conviction. The tendencies that this group represent are directly in line with the general change that has taken place in the moral actions of the modern generation. The one exception is that the percentage of those who had had sexual intercourse was not as high as one would expect. Even at that, however, the evidence that over one-fourth of them had had sex experience is sufficient to indicate a fairly high average of sophistication. More striking, however, is the one hundred percent reaction to the first part of the first question, and the approximately one hundred percent to the other part of the first question and to the second. The distinction between "necking" and "petting" was simply drawn: "Petting" stood for merely kissing and embracing, and "necking" for the more intimate varieties of caress. That almost all of the group participated in both of these types of affectionate endeavor, is at once to be noted. That more than five women were included in the circle of most of the men is also indicative of the extensiveness of their amorous approaches *and also of the freedom manifest on the part of the girls in providing such spontaneity of response.* The percentage of adultery was not unexpectedly small, because the tendency of these young men, most of them unmarried, to have relations with married women was on the average far less likely than that they would have them with the unmarried. More important, however, is the evidence in reference to the contacts of these men with houses of prostitution, and we shall discuss this later in connection with a detailed consideration of this angle of the problem.

In commenting upon these answers, one of the men,

who had been one of the protagonists in the project, added that it was clear that among the whole group, as among the younger generation at large, the old idea "that chastity was essential to a successful marriage" has receded if not entirely disappeared. In general conversations he found that everywhere among the youths that he met, in college and out, there was a consensus of agreement as to the wide change in moral habits and ethical standards. The change, in the eyes of these men, was from "dogmatic and absolute to esthetic and relative standards." Young people to-day, he maintained further, "are more inclined to have regard for demonstrable results rather than an abstract concept of sin." These observations are certainly tenable from the statistics supplied by the investigations undertaken. They are surely typical of the new attitude of youth.

A more thorough study of erotic attitudes and sexual expression was made by Drs. Peck and Wells, and the conclusions were embodied in their report entitled "A Study in the Psycho-Sexuality of College Graduate Men." One hundred men were included in the examination, but wherever answers were indefinite or dubious they were discounted. Thirty-seven per cent of the men admitted having had sexual intercourse prior to marriage. While this average is not as high as one would expect, one can say that the freedom with which these men, as all young men of today, were able to express themselves in necking and petting parties afforded a certain element of relief that under different conditions would have led them to the prostitute, and thus raised the average. It should also be noted here, that this average is singularly below that noted by other investigations and other observers. The statements as to the year in which they first had their sexual experience is of exceptional interest.

Here is the question, and the reply in percentage:
Question: *At what age did you first have intercourse, being not married:*

YEARS			YEARS		
10	....	o	18	....	5%
11	....	½%	19	....	6½%
12	....	o	20	....	4%
13	....	½%	21	....	5½%
14	....	1%	22	....	½%
15	....	4%	23	....	1%
16	....	2%	24	....	1%
17	....	4½%	25	....	1%

That the first rise in average should be at the age of fifteen is not puzzling at all. It is at that age, or a year earlier, that most boys find their interest in sex become a sudden, dynamic thing, and it is for that reason that the years of fourteen and fifteen, and in many cases thirteen, as we shall show in the next chapter, are marked by active recourse to auto-erotic practices, in particular masturbation. It is natural that where sex-relations are possible, masturbation will not be preferred. Youth becomes explorative at this period, and the fact that only 4% achieved intercourse at this age, and only 6½% at nineteen, is due not so much to moral compunction as to inexperience in approach, lack of opportunity, or difficulty of persuasion. The small average at 16 can be interpreted as a peculiarity of the group. The rise from 4½% at seventeen to 5% at eighteen and 6½% at nineteen is again a logical ascent. By those years youth has already increased his contacts, and the degree of awkwardness and unsophistication have been somewhat decreased. The potency of the sex-drive also has become more intensified. The years 20 and 21 show a slight variation that is not unusual in a group that has been exposed to diverse and complicated environments. The decrease after 21 was to be expected.

Other questions that were asked and which have pertinence to our analysis, were as follows:

Question: *Indicate by underscoring the approximate number of such episodes (sexual intercourse) up to the present time* (81% of the men were born in 1901).

Less than 10	10 to 20	21 to 40	41 to 60
20%	10%	11%	½%
61 to 80	81 to 100	Over 100	
1%	......	1%	

Question: *With how many different women have you had intercourse?*

1	2	3	4	5	More than 5
7.7%	3.6%	4.8%	3.1%	6.7%	10%

The replies to the first question are normal. That a large percentage of young men would be limited in the number of sex episodes is not an astonishing revelation, and among college graduates of this type such limitations, it may be added, very often result primarily from relations with more than five women, and 6.7% with five, and only 7.7% with only one, indicates something of pronounced significance.

Let us turn to an examination of 1000 unmarried women that was carried on by Dr. Davis, and see what it reveals in connection with our study. Of these 1000 women only 288 denied having had any experience with sexual intercourse, homosexuality or masturbation. 53 did not answer at all. 659 of these women, then, admitted having had one form or another, some all three, of these sex experiences. 603 of them stated that they had practiced masturbation. 184 admitted having had homosexual relations with physical expression. And 105 answered that they had had sexual intercourse. 289, therefore, had had either homosexual experience or sexual intercourse. The results of this questionnaire are extraordinarily instructive. They show, to begin with, that at most only three in every ten unmarried women are innocent of all sexual experience. The myth of the *pure* woman is rapidly fading into a recollection. While she often may not express her nature in the overt form of sex-contact, she certainly is not free of other practices, and, above all, if she does marry, she does not come to her husband, as the Victorian girl, with the ignorance of innocence as a token of her virtue.

These questionnaires certainly cannot be accepted as final. All study of change in contemporary morals, however, leads us to believe that their evidence errs more in the direction of understatement than overstatement. They are but an index to the change that is upon us. Most of the women questioned, as we previously observed, belong to the generation before the war. The new generation would show far more revolutionary changes.

The studies and statistics of Lindsey are more valuable, as we can readily appreciate, because they deal with the present generation, insurgent youth in its contemporary revolt. Those statistics that were largely concerned with men and women of the previous generation are of meaning in pointing out the earlier phase of this reaction before it became an actual revolt. The decay of modern marriage and the development of these new morals are intimately related. The growth of freer sexual relations on the part of youth has reduced the purely biological necessity of marriage for women as well as men. The sacredness of marriage has naturally vanished under these conditions of chaos. The new morality has brought us to a new cross-road in the history of morals in our civilization. Yet its actual realization can only be achieved in a new economic order.

CHAPTER VI

THE EFFECT OF CONTRACEPTIVES UPON FEMININE MORALS

AN important factor in the growth of the new morality, and the decay of modern marriage, has been the advancing perfection of modern contraceptives. A considerable part of the feminine revolt against the old morals has been fortified by this advance. Even the economic independence of the modern woman could not have established the new morality, with its contempt for chastity as an element in feminine virtue, and its advocacy of a freer attitude toward sex relations and alliances, if the danger of pregnancy was always imminent. Even feminine youth would not have carried its revolt so far had the drastic consequences of conception been unavoidable.

It has been the invention of modern contraceptives—and to a less extent modern prophylactics—that has fortified the challenge of youth with increasing vigor and security. The new morality and the spreading knowledge of contraceptives are closely associated. This does not mean that the revolt of youth and the rise of the new morals have been dependent upon the existence of contraceptive devices for their expression, but that the existence of these devices has aided the progress of these new attitudes by affording a protection from those consequences that would expose them to the attack of custom and convention. The existence of these attitudes of revolt arise from origins other than the invention of mechanical device or the concoction of chemical spermaticides. These contraceptive devices and concoctions, however, have accelerated the progress of the new attitude. Without them they might have been gradual, even tardy in their growth. With them, their growth has been rapid, electrically swift.

With the increasing use of contraceptives, the sex relation has rapidly changed in its emphasis. Regardless of the intention or desire of the individuals, the sex act has been insistently and inevitably associated with procreation. It was the procreative aspect, after all, that lent so much seriousness to the experience. Even in the case of Stanislavsky and Isadora Duncan, for instance, it was the element of the child, its imminent possibility, that deterred their union. In this case the positions were reversed. It

was the man who was more timid than the woman.
In most cases, however, it has been the woman who
has feared the danger of conception. This fear on
the part of woman was very natural indeed. It was
she who had to confront the world with the consequences that pursue such defections from established
virtue. It was she who had to bear the child, and, if
a little support was granted her, it was but a small
compensation for the social obloquy which she had
to suffer. As long as the procreative phase of the
sexual act remained in the ascendant, there was little
chance for emotional spontaneity between the sexes
to assert itself in other than the very superficial flir-
tation and caress. Although woman's plunge into the
economic world made her more independent, it did
not equip her sufficiently to combat all the costs of
pregnancy, childbirth, and child-rearing which were
implicit in the hazards of a freer sex life. It was only
the development of effective birth control methods
that could remove this fear, and shift the emphasis
in sex life from the procreational to the recreational.
Economic advance has given new resolve and courage,
and the challenge of independent personality; contraceptives have fortified this advance by removing from
the sex act the inequalities which at one time seemed
inherent and unavoidable in it. When sex can be-

come recreation without fear of procreation, it has at length, in our modern age, found a chance for a new release of energy and impulse. Women now have no more—or, if we wish, since it is true that birth-control has not become a perfect science, we may certainly say little more—to fear than men. Sex freedom holds no Damocles-sword over them to intimidate and terrify their recalcitrancy.

Marriage thus is rapidly coming to lose sexual significance for women as well as men. The sexual element in life can be satisfied outside of marriage and without many of the impediments which the marital life enforces upon the man as well as the woman. While this logic may not as yet be pursued by the mass, it has become part of the prevailing attitude of youth, and it certainly has become increasingly characteristic of the woman who seeks to live a life free of the trammels of domestic existence in order to achieve individual success and the distinction of a career.[1] Divorce has consequently become more at-

---

[1] Several of the reports and questionnaires that have been gathered have illustrated, in statistical form, the direct effect of the knowledge, of birth control methods upon the increasing freedom in feminine morality. Among the 71 women who had sexual intercourse before marriage, fifty, or 11.1 possessed information as to methods of contraception, and only nineteen, or 3.2% were ignorant of such knowledge. This is an arresting contrast. That these 71 women were less conventional than the other 929 is obvious without argument.

tractive as the advantages of married life have decreased in value and appeal.

Marriage after all is said, is an outgrowth of the
family, and not the family of marriage. With the
obvious disintegration of the family, which is noted by
everyone, marriage, for some time has lost its genuine meaning. Contraceptives have rapidly made
childless marriages very numerous. In our own day,
with the family reduced to a state of decay, and youth
concerned more with how to avoid than create children, marriage has become more and more meaningless. As a genuflection to convention, and a convenience to escape social embarrassments and stigmas,
it has continued, as a form or fiction. Without question, it has been the advancing perfection of contraceptives, in their capacity to avoid, as well as control
the number of children, which has provided a serious
menace to the marital institution.

If among these 71, those that violated the conventions were in the
majority of instances those who were acquainted with contraceptive
measures, it is not unlikely that this acquaintanceship played an important if not always a determining part in their sexual behavior.
Of course, no deductions could be safely made from such a small
group of women. Nevertheless, there is a strong likelihood that a
correlation may readily be found between the frequency of sex relations outside of marriage and awareness of birth-control technique. It
is because of this that this finding of Dr. Davis is at least sugges-
tive if not significant.

[123]

In this swirl of change, which has made the ready acceptance of contraceptives a conspicuous characteristic of our new generation, there is another factor that should not be neglected; namely, the decline of the supernatural outlook upon life and the rise of the scientific. While many people today still ascribe themselves to one religious creed or another the awe-inspiring influence of religion has largely disappeared, and the superstitious notions inculcated by its earlier prophets, with the advance of modern science, have been mainly abandoned. The fear of eternal damnation at least has lost its terrifying influence and moral power. Modern youth, for instance, is much more concerned about the physical injuries and ills that may follow its sexual adventures than it is with the spiritual. The philippics of the preacher do not frighten the modern boy and girl into virtue. The prevalence of spicy slang[2] alone counteracts any intrusion of religious inspiration into ordinary discourse or conversation. If religion sometimes continues in the home, it certainly does not spread into the dance hall, club room and various societies organized by youth for sport and pleasure. And with the entire institution of the home in rapid decay, its influence there is unlasting and negligible.

[2] George Jean Nathan's "The Land of the Pilgrim's Pride."

The older generation is being superseded by a newer. The ignorance of birth control methods is being rapidly erased. The youth of today, and boys and girls who have become men and women in the present generation, have become rapidly sophisticated in such methods. Many of them have learned, through *bootleg* literature and *bootleg* instruction, some through casual contacts, some from their elders, the ways of tasting joy without its old penalties and pains. This knowledge, the details of which questionnaires among the younger generation may later reveal, has unquestionably functioned as a factor in the rise of these new morals.

In America this knowledge must be concealed from the public. The concealment, however, is but an ironic farce. While the older set may be uninformed as to the achievements of contraceptive science, the younger is certainly aware of its cruder methods if not its subtler. The modern youth who is uncognizant of at least one method of birth-control, is either an anomaly or a curious case of moral senility settling upon a young head. A further illustration of the extent with which contraceptives are used by those not of the new generation is to be found in another report of Dr. Davis. Among 1000 women who were questioned as to their attitude toward, and use of, contraceptives, we find that 730 are employing them and that only 78 express disapproval of their use. 520 of these 730 women are university and college graduates, 47 are college undergraduates, 102 are high and normal school graduates, 40 are those who have had less than a high school education, and 21 are those who have been tutored in private schools or by private instructors. Over 75% of these 1000 women, for instance, in statistical enumeration, approve of voluntary parenthood, which means that they approve of the idea of birth control, and therefore, of the employment of contraceptives. In the meanwhile, we refuse to repeal a law that forbids the dissemination of scientific knowledge of birth-control, oppose the organization of clinics that would purpose to advance such knowledge, and, in so doing, foster the spread of unscientific information and the increase of disease and death.

The invention of means to prevent conception is not a novel or recent achievement. Even the primitives resorted to contraceptive measures in the course of their sexual life. While these means very often extended to the extremes of mutilation, such as the method called *mika* which is practiced among the tribes in Australia, their effectiveness is not to be disputed. In fact, they reveal an exceptional cleverness and ingenuity for that stage in man's development. When we remember that there were certain primitive tribes that were unaware of the causal relationship which existed between sexual intercourse, pregnancy, and child-birth, it is certainly with interest verging on wonder that we observe other tribes that have made definite advance in the artifice of contraception. The first mechanical contraceptives were used in China many years ago, but it is not until the thirteenth century that the contraceptive is invented in the west. Fallopius, the leading anatomist of the sixteenth century, recommended their use. First utilized in Italy, it was not long before they became known in France and England. Casanova, for instance, scorned their use as crude and inexquisite. The remarks of Voltaire and Madame de Sévigné upon their indelicacy are familiar to those who know the intimate letters of that period. In England, they were well-known to the courtiers of Charles II. Their costliness, however, prevented their use on any but a very inextensive scale. Only the upper classes could purchase them, and even with these groups, as we have seen, they were not widely utilized. It was not until the nineteenth century that contraceptives became used by other than a limited few. Even then their scale was not wide. It was only gradually that their existence became known to the populace. Their purchase, however, still remained beyond the economic capacity of the commoner. They were a luxury resorted to by those who could afford it. Toward the end of the nineteenth century, however, with more markets from which to draw materials, their cost of production was sharply reduced, and manufacture on the large scale became feasible. Decrease in selling price soon effected an increase in sales. Then, too, with large scale production their forms could be more diversified, and differences in quality could meet differences in economic capacity to purchase. Even at that their retail price never became so low as to convert them into an unextravagant utility.

It was the War again that caused a sudden and decisive change in the history of their use and influence. Before the War their existence had not reached the ears of the entire populace. The foreign elements in the country that had not yet assimilated American virtues, perhaps, had not learned of their efficacy. Youths often grew up in ignorance of their existence, but more often it was with knowledge of their nature confined to pictorial and verbal forms. The War changed all this. As we described in earlier chapters, the War accelerated the destruction of the older ideals. Conservative attitudes were galvanized into their revolutionary opposites under the fire of shot and shell. The sex insanity upon the stage as we pointed out in our earlier treatment of the effects of the War, was one indication of how Paris met the demands of the soldier. The thousands of prophylactic stations, with their lines stretching into the hundreds of thousands, men returning from leave and furlough, was conspicuous testimony of the sex activity of the soldier. The moral psychology of the populations that remained at home also suffered electrical shock and transformation.

In order to fortify this observation with fact, I have made a reasonably close study of the manufacture and sale of contraceptives in Baltimore. While Baltimore may not represent the average city in the United States, its deviations from type are not enormous. Indeed, its dull conservatism in political attitude, its unperturbed slowness if not economy of effort in the ordinary procedure of life, its lack of adventurousness and fear of progress—it may be that these factors tend to make it fall below the average, in revealing the nature of this change in morals that has swept across this country as well as across the rest of the western world. At all events, considering the possibilities of divergence from norm, Baltimore is certainly a city sufficiently large in proportions (over 800,000 population) to convey some of the more manifest changes that have occurred in this generation. At least, it will give us a clue as to the extensity of the phenomenon now under our scrutiny.

After a careful study of the sale and distribution of contraceptives in the drug-stores of Baltimore, it is a reasonable estimate that over 2,250,000 contraceptives are sold by them each year. Besides the sale through drug-stores, there is an equally if not far more enormous traffic in the same goods, carried on through the agency of the grocery store, confectionery shop, dry goods establishment, and the general pedlar. How widespread this traffic is one can appreciate only when he has come into contact with a wholesale distributor of his wares. Every type of store practically, from grocery to confectionery, is included within the scope of his distribution. In addition to this distribution of contraceptive materials to stores of all types, there are hundreds of jobbers working at the same business. These small jobbers, in many cases, older boys who undertake the work for the sake of a small remuneration, sell either to stores not convassed by the wholesale distributor, or directly to the consumer. In the latter endeavor alone there is a stupendous profit. Such salesmen are prolific in every modern city. In Baltimore, for instance, it is estimated that there are at least two hundred of them who earn their entire living from this trade.

At this point, we wish to emphasize certain evidence that is of importance in the growth of the new morality and the War. At no time before had there been this immense expansion of the business of manufacturing, distributing, and selling contraceptives as is to be noted with the War. At no time before had there been such knowledge of, and such interest in, contraceptives, nor had their purchase ever been at all phenomenal. The War spun the wheel in the reverse direction. What before was merely a profitable business, now became a matter for large-scale production, with the development of all the details of distribution centers, smaller distribution centers, with large jobbers and small jobbers, salesmen, and all of the paraphernalia of an enormous industry.[3] While before the War the sale of this specific contraceptive, to which we have reference, totalled in a city like Baltimore a sale of two or three millions a year, since the War the total has leaped to probably as many as 6,250,000. These figures, it should be remembered, are confined to but one kind of contraceptive, which,

[3] In order to remove our calculations from the field of pure speculation, I have checked up all computations with the numerous agencies of distribution, which, in a matter so indefinite, was the closest approach to exactitude that could be made.

however, is the one most popular in use. Other contraceptives of varying types and costliness are surprisingly numerous. Since the varieties differ so widely, however, with one agency selling this kind and another that, the scale of sales is difficult to garner and averages almost impossible to compute.

The ruling under which these contraceptives are sold is one of the most curious evasions of ethical legerdemain. It only indicates the essential hypocrisy of our moral standards. The laws against the sale of contraceptives can be escaped as easily as the laws that limit divorce. In the matter of divorce, collusion is a well-known and frequently utilized, if illegal method. The illegal can always be made legal when the price can be paid. It only needs a legal expert to introduce a little illegal magic, and the trick of transformation is achieved. In the matter of contraceptives, even the legal expert is not required. If contraceptives cannot be sold as contraceptives, certainly they can be sold under another name, and for another purpose. After all, this is not an unusual legal subterfuge. It is familiar in many other cases, and under many other aspects. That contraceptives, therefore, should be sold as prophylactics—despite the fact that there are a number of prophylactics—is not at all surprising. It is really an intelligent adaptation to an unintelligent morality and superstition.

Confronted with this situation, it is pathetic, nay, amusing with all of its tragedy, to consider the attitudes that exist toward the use of contraceptives and the general problem of birth control. I do not mean the attitude of the populace, which may often condemn the very practice it pursues, but that of the old generation, the medical profession, the moral intelligentzia. Perhaps no greater travesty upon human intelligence can be discovered at the present time. Certainly there is no better illustration of how intelligence is warped by traditions and institutions, how freedom is fettered by its dedication to the past.

Let us consider some of the more obvious aspects of this travesty. In no medical school that I have been able to discover, is the subject of contraceptives studied. With the people at large resorting to the practice, the doctor is educated in total ignorance of the methods and science of birth-control. Medical schools avoid the topic. Whatever knowledge of birth control a physician possesses he must acquire outside of educational institutions. There is nothing scientific about this knowledge. The books on the topic are obscure and evasive. In one medical school in New York I have been informed, a professor, who was courageous enough to attempt to give a brief lecture on birth-control, and its methods of application, requested that the girls leave the class while this lecture was rendered. This request was ridiculous. Yet other medical schools would not even hazard such a lecture at all. Medical men—or shall we call them modern medicine men—brought up in ignorance of one of the most important phenomena in the personal life of the contemporary individual!

It is no wonder, then, that the attitude toward birth-control and sex-instruction, is as stupid as medieval superstition.[4] The replies to a questionnaire sent

[4] The following instance, described by Prof. Harry Elmer Barnes ("The Social Basis of Mental Hygiene," *Survey*, Jan. 15, 1928) portrays the prevailing attitude:

" 'To investigate the social basis of mental health implies a secular and experimental attitude toward human society, whereas in the past the conventional and respectable approach has been the supernatural or religious, which focusses upon the protection of man from the Devil or evil spirits, or upon fitting an immortal soul for the world to come.' Many groups of scientists, natural, psychological and social, are at work amassing information as to the nature of man and his social setting, and it is very likely that they will not be able to provide rational guidance for human behavior before we are sufficiently free of the religious fixation to be willing to accept it. When the essentials of this article were presented before the Pennsylvania and All-Philadelphia Conference of Social Work some months ago a psychiatrist followed the present writer on the program. I had mentioned neither the Seventh Commandment nor Freud, but this speaker commented in apparent indignation and excitement. 'The sooner we get back to the Seventh Commandment instead of substituting Freud in our homes for the Bible, the better we will be off.'

out by Drs. John B. Watson and K. S. Lashley, on the topic of Sex Education, reveal the abysmal absurdity of this attitude.[5]   This questionnaire was sent out to 39 doctors of the American Psychopathological Association, 18 surgeons of the American Association of Genito-Urinary Surgeons, 12 physicians of the American Gynecological Society.   In answer to the question:

Should members of either sex or both sexes be instructed before marriage in the physiology and psychology of sexual intercourse?

Only 25 gave unqualified approval.   44, then, disapproved.   The unintelligence manifest in this disapproval is illustrated in the answers of Dr. Baldy: "No, only excites our curiosity.   Can see no possible good to offset that fact.   Dr. Hugh Cabot: "Such teaching is highly risky business, and I am unwilling to assent to it at present"; and the single answer of Dr. Jeanette Sherman: "No."   In reference to the question:

The good doctor did not stop to explain just why Moses should be regarded as a more reliable authority on adultery than on dementia-praecox, though we may express a modest doubt as to whether he still resorts to a practice of exorcising devils in treating his patients."

[5] "Consensus of Medical Opinion upon Questions Relating to Sex Education and Venereal Disease Campaigns."   J. B. Watson and L. S. Lashley—*Medical Hygiene,* October, 1920.

Should the anatomy and physiology of the organs of the opposite sex be taught?

Thirty gave their unqualified negative response. Such idiotic recommendation of ignorance in the cause of virtue is unspeakably tragic.

In answer to another question:

Should details of ovulation, impregnation, and the development of the embryo be taught, or should instruction be limited to the external manifestations of pregnancy and personal hygiene?

Three actually voted for no instruction at all, and 39 for limited instruction to external manifestations only.

When the spirit and sentiment of these reactions are understood, the attitude toward birth control can be immediately predicted. In the answers to the questionnaire submitted to the members of the New York Obstetrical Society,[6] the following replies are signal:

In response to the general desire for an expression of opinion by authorative medical organizations on the subject popularly known as birth control, do you approve of a scientific study of this topic sponsored by this Society?

Fifteen out of the 57 replied definitely in the negative, and 14 did not answer.

[6] See above note on this report.

Do you give instructions immediately preceding marriage?

Fifteen unequivocally stated "no," 17 said "occasionally" and seven did not answer.

Do you believe that special clinics should be established, devoted to this purpose (instruction in birth-control and nature of child-birth) and manned by physicians and nurses?

Thirty-four answered unambiguously in the negative.

When we reflect upon the nature of these answers, despair deepens. We are in the grip of a fearful narrow-mindedness that has grown out of a ridiculous code of ascetic morals. If these answers were given by preachers, their conservatism might have been anticipated. But that 15 obstetricians should disapprove of sponsoring a scientific study of birth control; that 16 should not give, or refuse to give, instruction for those just about to be married; and that 34 should oppose the idea of special clinics organized for the purpose of sex-instruction—such attitudes are insanely conservative.

More revealing still are the answers to the question:

Should information concerning contraceptives be made generally accessible to the public?

Only 4 answered yes, and 42 declared themselves definitely opposed to the idea. Seven gave varying answers, difficult to classify, and four did not answer in any way whatsoever.

That 42 obstetricians, psychopathologists, and surgeons, should desire the public to be kept in ignorance of the scientific knowledge of contraceptives, when they are already cognizant of the fact that the public purchases them in a wide-spread manner, and is only unaware of the science underlying their manifold applications—that obstetricians could express such an unenlightened and unprogressive attitude would be incredible were it not for our understanding of how scientific minds are enslaved by moral and religious tradition. The stupidity of this attitude becomes increasingly apparent when we return for another glance at the calculated sale of contraceptives in one city such as Baltimore. If these men, because of their profession, do not prefer to repeat the story of the stork, they surely have not advanced beyond the one of the ostrich.[7]

[7] In England the report of British doctors is not less absurd and unscientific. (Continence in Relation to Social Hygiene—a statement prepared by the British Social Hygiene committee and adopted by the British Social Hygiene council at their meeting on March 22, 1926. *Journal of Social Hygiene*.) Their defense of chastity is as convincing, despite its appeal to scientific terminology, as an ecclesiastical sermon. Their conclusions apropos of sexual continence and

While in Holland, Germany, England, and Soviet Russia, birth control clinics have been established, in the United States their organization is a mere fiction. In reference to the matter of voluntary parenthood, their attitude is ossified by religious tradition. Information as to contraception is given only to those representing extremely exigent cases and especially sent to the clinic by *reputable* physicians. In Europe, advice and instruction are given without the compulsion of emergency. In two clinics in England, that of Stopes and Walworth's Women's Welfare Center, over 13,000 cases have been handled within the last six years. In Holland, Germany, Ireland, Scandinavia, thousands of cases have been treated with intelligent advice and instruction. In America, on the contrary, the American Birth Control League reports that 80 letters are received a day, applying for information as to contraceptives, (one doctor out of every eight in America makes such an application), and that 28,384 of such

sexual restraint, with reference to Arctic explorers and whalers, are about as realistic as a fish yarn. Their hope, that "all illicit relations, whether before or after marriage, will be recognized as contrary to man's higher nature," is an amusing reflection that is as removed from reality as a hashish dream. Unfortunately, the higher nature of man in the past, particularly when it has expressed itself in the form of genius, was a very contrary and contradictory thing. The comments of these eminent doctors upon convicts, and their achievement of "man's higher nature" through coercion, gives the final touch of melodrama to their parade of piffle.

letters had been received up until July 1926, and furthermore, that 1,341 persons had applied in person for such information. These requests can only be met by evasive suggestions or private instruction taken at the risk of imprisonment. Consequently, despite the requests of thousands for scientific information, their unscientific practices must be perpetuated in order to protect the superstitious spirit of the ruling order.

The argument of Dr. Sutherland in England that birth-control should be fought, because it spells race-suicide; or that of the Rev. J. Barr, a labor member in Parliament, that instruction in the methods of birth control means instruction in "a policy of despair"; or that of the Right Reverend John A. Ryan in America that "self-respect and mutual respect" are destroyed by the introduction of contraceptives—these arguments are but part of the logic of the old generation. The response of the populace is not in their favor. Youth sneers at them. Nature's excesses must be checked. We check them in the external world. Why should we not check them in the internal? Birth control is but another way that human intelligence has devised to exercise a check upon nature's will to wildness.

When statisticians and moralists point out to them the decline of birth-rate in the western world, and the danger that it harbingers for the white race—that the number of children entering the schools in England and Wales was fewer by 100,000 in 1926; [8] that Germany's birth-rate has been reduced from an average of 35 per 1000 in 1900 to 20.4 per 1000 in 1924; that France's birth-rate of 21.3 in 1900 had declined to 19.4 in 1924; [9] that in Vienna the deaths exceeded the living births by 2,303, and that in the whole of Austria this excess of deaths over births totalled 28,220[10]—their reply is not one of alarm or fear. It is better that the world be saved from the burden of an enormous population; it is better that unwanted children should not be born; it is better that the birth-rate decline, if happiness and joy multiply—this is their answer.

In my study of the sale of contraceptives in Baltimore, I found that, on the average, at least 50% of those who purchased contraceptives were unmarried. Of course, to establish such a figure with precision, is' impossible. All I could depend upon were the observations of those connected with the sale of these materials. In certain cases, although the average was not high, girls were active in their purchase. That the

[8] *Journal of American Medical Association.* Dec. 18, 1926.
[9] *Ibid.*, Vol. 87—July 31, 1926.
[10] *Ibid.*, Oct. 29, 1927.

use of contraceptives among the unmarried is a wide-spread practice, everyone acquainted with modern morals and modern youth will affirm. Now that contraceptives can be bought in grocery store as well as confectionery shop, they present no difficulty to purchase. Dr. Lewellys Barker, professor Emeritus of Medicine at the Johns Hopkins University, stated in a lecture at the University of Washington last summer that:

> "The young people are in a modified way having trial marriages. The ease with which contraceptives are purchased at cigar-stores has given youth a false sense of security·from possible infection and conception, and in the absence of any idealism about marriage and home many have in their own language gone the limit." [11]

Girls and women today, then, can disdain virtue because its absence does not induce ruin. The advance of birth-control methods has been an important and determining factor in their new reaction. The statistics alone which we cited at the beginning of this chapter indicate the tendency of women to admit greater freedoms with the protection of the contraceptive, and to find in the contraceptives themselves

[11] Quoted from an article by Mabel Seagrave (M.D.), "Causes Underlying Sex Delinquency in Young Girls," *Journal of Social Hygiene.* Vol. 2, 1926.

a solution to dangers that at one time seemed inescapable. If sex relations were still as fraught with
the danger of pregnancy as in earlier centuries, part
of our new-born sex freedom would have been short-
lived. With the fear of pregnancy largely eliminated,
however, it is no longer only the rich who can afford
to be immoral. As yet contraceptives are not so cheap
that the proletariat can purchase them without economic handicap, but they are rapidly reaching that
level. Youths, nevertheless, of all classes, can manage
to secure them for their sundry adventures and esca-
pades. In the days of the aristocracies, the nobility
could be free in its morals, because it could afford the
existence of mistresses and bastards, and the other
consequences of a loose and licentious life. The conflict between the sexual impulse and the restrictions of
a moral code is usually solved by the victory of the
former when violations of the latter can be achieved
without distress or pain. For a long time only the
wealthy could afford these violations. Now, with the
invention of modern contraceptives, these violations
have lost their seriousness and gravity. They can
be undertaken by the multitude. Youth's explora-
tiveness can be expressed with impunity.

In other words, while the inconvenience of a pregnancy, and the handicap of a child, were difficulties

once too sombre to hazard, the introduction of the contraceptive, by minimizing their danger, has reduced the value of virtue. Or virtue, if you please, has spritely assumed the colors of a chameleon.

CHAPTER VII

COMPANIONATE MARRIAGE AND THE SEXUAL IMPULSE

COMPANIONATE marriage is one of the newest suggestions that has been proposed as a solution to the present moral chaos of youth. As we have seen, part of the revolt in the direction of greater sex freedom has been due to the decay of modern marriage and the contempt with which youth has come to regard the marital institution. The dissemination of knowledge of birth-control technique, as we now know, has exercised a decisive influence in the development of this attitude. The decline of religion, also, which is but part of the general bankruptcy of the old system of ideals and concepts, has aided in the formulation of this new outlook. The sacred today, as a result of the changes we have recorded, has been replaced by the practical. While no one would argue that the practical was ignored by our ancestors, at the same time it must not be forgotten that that was in the days when traffic in the sacred was part of the serious business of life. Now the sacred is less popular. In the old days the practical was hallowed by the religious. Today youth and the young generation in general do not require holiness to justify their virtues or the concept of sin to condemn their vices. The present attitude is more pragmatic. Marriage is a practical thing—an experience in human relationship that more often proves one of vice than virtue. Those who still continue to parade its sanctity—on platform or pulpit—the new generation greets with derision.

Companionate marriage, as suggested by Judge Lindsey, is no radical or revolutionary gesture. In fact it would be nothing more than an interesting attempt to institutionalize a trial and error experiment. It would legalize what is now illegal, and conventionalize by statute what rapidly is becoming an illicit convention. It is Judge Lindsey's aim to introduce companionate marriage as a means of saving the marital institution from entire disintegration. What is companionate marriage? We shall let Judge Lindsey explain his own idea.

"Companionate marriage, as I conceive it, as it has been explained time and time again by sociologists, and as it has been discussed for years in the pages of the *Journal of Social Hygiene,* one of our outstanding sociological publications, is a state of lawful wedlock, entered into for love, companionship, and coöperation by persons who, for reasons of health, finances, temperament, etc., are not prepared at the time of their marriage to undertake the care of a family.

"If this form of marriage were recognized by law, people who entered it would *openly* profess their intention not to have children without special license from the state; and the state would instruct them in scientific birth control, to that end. It would also instruct them, in a House of Human Welfare, about the meaning and significance of sex, and in the art of love, to the end that they might enter marriage with some knowledge of how to avoid the pitfalls of ignorance, prudery, and other things which wreck many a marriage." [1]

There is really nothing new in this idea at all, except that it provides for official instruction in birth control for those participating in the alliance, and for freedom of divorce upon the basis of mutual consent, in the absence of progeny, if the parties later decide to separate. But Judge Lindsey recognizes this fact, and on another page states that he is only "proposing to legalize what you now have illegally." Later on he adds:

"Companionate marriage . . . is widely practiced by thousands of perfectly respectable, legally married people today. You and I both know scores of childless couples. They have most of them decided not to have children, and they have a perfect right so to decide. It is a personal

[1] "Companionate Marriage," by Judge Lindsey. Page 175.

matter. No stigma of immorality attaches to these marriages or to yours. Society recognizes them as moral and permissible. But the recognition is tacit. Society thinks it shocking if anybody suggests that the regulations governing this kind of marriage be adapted to the practical necessities of such union, and that if this were done the Companionate Marriage could be made a powerful instrument, both for social reform and for human happiness.

"Now let me point out to you one thing about these childless marriages that you may not have thought of. Deliberately childless marriages involve, in ninety-nine cases out of a hundred, the use of contraceptives. But this involves a violation of the law that forbids the manufacture and sale of contraceptives and the imparting of contraceptive information. Since this use of contraceptives is against the law, deliberate childlessness is also against the law whenever it involves the use of these illegal contraceptives. This is a form of law-violation which people practice as a matter of course, without scruple. It is winked at by the authorities; and it amounts to a nullification of one of the craziest pieces of freak legislation ever put over in this country. This is a fact. Childless marriages usually involve bootleg Birth Control. And *yet* these marriages, childless by means of utterly illegal agencies, and by a technically felonious breaking of the law, are recognized by church, state, and society as perfectly respectable; and no stigma attaches to persons who so marry and so conduct themselves in marriage."

With the attitude manifest on the part of the moral and political intelligence of the ruling groups in the United States today, companionate marriages in the near future may multiply in secret but they will not be sanctioned in public. Birth control methods may become the knowledge of every youth and be practiced by every couple, but they will not be approved by moral custom.[2] Hypocrisy and deception are still precious attributes in our moral scheme of things. We

[2] The power of the Church is not the only obstacle to the introduction of birth control as a measure of social intelligence. This attitude, after all, is rooted in the Christian concept of sex as a sin. In an individual such as Dr. Howard Kelly, for instance, who is a Protestant and not a Catholic, and who as scientist and professor in the Johns Hopkins Medical School, and as a contributor to the cure of cancer by radium is an internationally known figure, we find a striking illustration of the kind of attitude which prevails toward morals and sex. This Dr. Kelly devoted much of his energy recommending that all physicians become Christians. Not many years ago also it was he who strenuously opposed the idea of disseminating freely information as to venereal prophylactics for fear that the tendency to promiscuous sexual intercourse would then be augmented. Another instance of the prevailing attitude was evinced in connection with the recent attempt to organize a Birth Control Clinic under the auspices of the Johns Hopkins Hospital. The mere announcement of this endeavor evoked such bitter and extreme attack that while the effort has not been abandoned, it has been forced to operate in a quiet and almost clandestine manner. This Birth Control clinic is to have none of the characteristics that Lindsey would desire it to possess. This clinic only handles cases that are duly sent to it by physicians. There is nothing radical about its program. Yet the very word Birth Control is sufficient to stimulate opposition so vigorous that even such a clinic, as we see, is driven to semi-concealment.

exalt them under other appellations. Our predicament is amusingly verbal. We convince ourselves that our methods are moral so long as their terminology does not violate the old conventions. We pass a law, as we saw in a preceding chapter, preventing the sale of contraceptive materials, but allow these same materials to be sold in order to prevent the contraction of disease. Thus we practice what we disapprove under a name that we approve.

While companionate marriage can never solve the sex problem nor be anything else than a mere patch upon the face of a volcano, the interest that it has awakened has brought to light a certain discrepancy in sex life which has usually been obscured by euphemism and evasion. That companionate marriage has already become an illegal practice among the young is of more significance to our consideration than the earnest endeavors of Lindsey to convert it into a legal institution. Its illegal existence, of course, is but another expression of revolt against the system of uncompanate marriage, which is evidenced in the decay and bankruptcy of modern marriage in general, and a further expression of the new morality in active form.

In coming to more direct grip with the sexual problem, what companionate marriage fundamentally reveals is the prepotency of the purely biological over the purely economic. The disparity between the age at which the young are able to marry and the age at which their sexual system becomes active, has been the cause of untold suffering and distress. With the development of the economic life of modern industrial society this disparity has become deepened and aggravated. Marriage is financially impossible for most young couples before the early twenties, and even at that age it very often appears to be something of an economic hazard. If the moral ideal which our society exalted, that of continence outside the marital relation, was to be maintained it was only at the cost of indescribable suppression and suffering. Sexual appetencies were never created for economic "checks and balances." Sex desire as a normal, spontaneous thing does not wait on society to instruct it as to its time for expression. This conflict between the biological and the economic is too acute and significant to be observed by the moralist. It is a vital, destructive disparity. As an expression of industrial civilization, it has brought us to our neurotic age.

The revolutions in production achieved not only a transformation in the economic structure of the world; they achieved also new moral standards, new attitudes toward marriage, different notions toward sex, and a multiplying mass of situations that occasioned new adjustments in fashion too rapid for human change. The maladjustment of our modern world is an inevitable consequence. The sex attitude which received such direct emphasis with the rise of the puritanic bourgeoisie to power, which we previously described in detail, was an enormous incongruity. For over two centuries sex was viewed as unclean and sinful. While this attitude was in origin an outgrowth of the Christian concept of sex as a sin, it was not until the rise of the commercial classes in the seventeenth century that it became an all-pervasive doctrine. At one time supposed to be revered by priest, this attitude now was set up for the unvacillating reverence of all men. All life and literature became infected with it. Chastity became stressed as the *sine qua non* of feminine virtue. Because men were the owners and not the owned, this criterion became inviolable. The revolt of women in the twelfth century, when adultery became the fashion, was now part of an unholy past. For men, violations were not approved; in fact, for several generations they met with severe punishment, but as masculine impulse asserted itself against the restraints of this economical ethics, it soon took advantage of its position of privilege and gradually began to condone in men what in women remained the unpardonable sin. The double-code of morality thus grew up as a result of man's subordination of women in the organization of society, and allowed for him an escape that was closed for women. As generations advanced, for instance, the bachelor was never considered a celibate, although the spinster was always looked upon as sexually purer than a nun. This change, however, was part of a silent understanding that was never written into moral dogma or blessed as an open attribute of virtue. Nevertheless, in law it was protected by the difference in emphasis that was laid upon the act of adultery on the part of woman from that on the part of man. Its existence was undeniable.

This double-code of morality, which prevailed in the days of feminine dependence, became obvious in the proverb that every young man had "his wild oats to sow" before he got married, and this sowing was understood by women as well as men. Their acquiescence, as we have observed, was a sign of the beautiful submission that was the characteristic virtue of woman during this period. While this submission was exalted as an element of the sublime, and praised in poetry and prose, it was in reality but an expresion of sex-subordination in the moral world which had its immediate counterpart in the economic.

Although men thus had an opportunity for freedom in their sexual lives that was not possible for women, the growing boy did not learn of the elasticity of this masculine ethic until he had rapidly advanced toward manhood. Sex expression for girls, of course, was utterly forbidden outside marriage. As a consequence both sexes learned to suffer restraints and repressions that not only disturbed and agitated their immediate lives but also prevented their later existence from attaining an emotional equilibrium. The effects of these years of bitter sex-struggle often poisoned their entire existence in the future. Instead of developing into strong, balanced, excellent types of manhood and womanhood, they often became, on the other hand, uncertain, vacillating men and women adapted only to the pathological way of life of the neurotic. As men and women they could not escape their youth. Its cost had been too sharp and consuming. The multiplication of neurotics and psychotics in this age, the appalling increase in the insane, the spread of psychiatry as a science, the rise of Freud and Adler as diverse exemplars of its technique—all these attest the reality of this terrific maladjustment that has occurred in our civilization. While it is certainly true that the fundamental factor is the vast change from rural to urban life, and from individualistic production to mass production, with the consequent acceleration of the whole movement of life, the creation of

[154]

its industrial unrest, torture and chaos, and madness for profits, it must not be thought that the effect of this sweeping change in the evocation of conflict between economics and sex, is of unimportant and unrevolutionary character. The obsessing concern with sex today is a natural recoil from the repressions of the last nine or ten generations. Freud's emphasis upon sex as the explanation of all phenomena is but an exaggeration necessary to combat the sickening secrecy with which sex has been obscured in the past.

In the revolt of youth, connected as it is with the economic independence of modern woman, the bankruptcy of marriage, the decay of the bourgeoisie as a moral class, we have the dynamic beginnings of *The Sexual Revolution*.

One of the most interesting expressions of the deleterious effects that the old moral code inflicted upon youth, and very often extended through the life of mature men and women, is that of masturbation. Masturbation, of course, is not a new phenomenon. It can be found in primitive times and ancient as well as modern. In India, with the prevalence of superstition and taboo and an attitude toward sex which is as unhealthy as that of the west, masturbation has long been a widespread practice. Miss Mayo in her recent book "Mother India," endeavors to trace part of the essential weakness of the Hindu people to this source. While her conclusion in this reference, as in many others, is open to dispute, masturbation as a practice scarcely can be encouraged or recommended. If its effects upon the Hindus cannot be precisely defined, certainly they cannot be said to be beneficial. While in the past it may have been absurd to magnify the evil effects of masturbation upon the individual, it surely would not be a more intelligent tactic to ascribe to the habit today the elements of a virtue. That in most cases its effects are not obvious, and in many instances can be said to have made no apparent invasions upon the personality, in a great number of cases, as every psychiatrician will testify, its effects have been devastating and pernicious.

With modern civilization, in its attempt to curb the sexual impulse in order to make it fit into its ethical code and acquisitive economy, masturbation has become a common practice of youth. Masturbation is a manifestation of either deprivation of sex activity or dissatisfaction with the activity experienced. With youth, in the vast majority of cases, it is deprivation rather than dissatisfaction that is the cause of the habit. That women are often said to be more addicted to the habit than men is not surprising when we realize that as male youths mature into men the chances for gratification are, or at least were, more abundant than for girls who mature into women without marriage as a solution for their situation. Havelock Ellis' comment upon this fact is pertinent:

"After adolescence I think there can be no doubt that masturbation is more common in women than in men. Men have by this time mostly adopted some method of sexual gratification with the opposite sex; women are to a much larger extent shut off from such gratification." [3]

All investigations as to the habit of masturbation have revealed its excessive extensity. In a study of 948 college men, the largest group of cases statistically handled up to that time, 61.5% of the men admitted addiction to the habit.[4] Among a group of students taking extension courses at Columbia, thirty-nine men in all, 74.4% acknowledged their practice of masturbation, and of the thirty-one women, 45.2% confessed experience in the practice. If these percentages do not confirm the estimate of Osker Berger that 99% of both sexes masturbate, or that of Horace W. Funk that 90% practice the habit, they certainly support the several investigations made in Russia and Italy, the one in Italy conducted by Moraglia, that sixty per-

[3] "Studies in Psychology of Sex," Havelock Ellis.
[4] "Problems and Principles of Sex Education—A Study of 948 College Men." By Dr. Max Joseph Exnor. *N. Y. Associated Press.*

cent is an unexaggerated norm. The investigation of
Dr. Davis also confirmed the accuracy of this average.
Among the 1000 unmarried women included in this
study, 603, or 60.3%, admitted either having practiced masturbation or were still practicing it at the
time of the inquiry. Only 327, or 32.7% denied ever
having practiced it. Seventy failed to answer. Most
of the women involved were in their late twenties and
thirties; only four were under 25 years. One woman
was forty. 568 of them were teachers; 140 social
workers, 63 secretaries, 62 librarians, and only 46 had
never been employed in any earning capacity at all.
The group, therefore, was reasonably high in training
and intelligence. The sixty percent, as a consequence,
is perhaps lower, rather than higher than the actual
average among women as a whole.

Masturbation only	396
Sexual intercourse only	12
Homosexual experience only	43
Both masturbation and homosexual experiences	115
Both masturbation and sexual intercourse	67
Both sexual intercourse and homosexual experiences	61
Masturbation, sexual intercourse, and homosexual experiences	25
All these sex experiences denied	288
Questions relating to all these experiences unanswered	53
	1000

The above table discloses the autoerotic and heteroerotic experiences of these 1000 unmarried women.

When we begin to study this group more closely there are other characteristics that soon become manifest. In the first place the chart immediately below reveals a definite wave-rhythm that is not without meaning:

Age	Now Practicing	Stopped	Never Practiced
20–29	27.7	35.9	36.4
30–39	35.5	30.2	34.3
40–49	36.6	29.3	34.1
50–59	31.7	29.3	39.0
60–69	8.7	60.9	30.4

The first observation that is singularly conspicuous is that the cessation of practice among those already given to the habit is most marked between the years the tendency to masturbation, except among cases characterized by neurosis, would certainly diminish. It is only when these sexual contacts evoke severe dissatisfactions that they might tend to increase with practice. On the whole, however, it is far more likely that sex contacts during this period would tend to stop rather than stimulate the habit, which would explain, to an extent, the large number who stopped the practice during these years. (35.9%) Furthermore, after thirty is passed we note that the number who cease the habit becomes steadily less until we strike the senile-meridian, with menopause as the decisive factor. Among the group practicing the habit also we note an increase after thirty which continues until the age of fifty. At fifty, in most cases, menopause has already set in but has not completed its change, and consequently the decrease of 4.9% from the previous period is explained by the influence of menopause upon a certain number of cases, but it fails, at this time, to effect the sweeping change that is noted in the next decade. As we remarked before, with the on-coming of the sixties not only has menopause completed its revolution in feminine physiology but the process of superannuation in general has advanced with such startling rapidity that it is even surprising that 8.7% still continue the habit.

In the few studies of the ages at which the two sexes actually begin masturbation, we are able to detect differences that are of value to an understanding of the sex-life. From the investigations of Drs. Peck and Wells, we find that the age at which most boys begin their onanistic practices is at 13, 14 and 15;[5] from the inquiries of Dr. Davis among her group of a 1000

---

[5] "On the Psycho-Sexuality of College Graduate Men." M. W. Peck and F. L. Wells. Boston Psychopathic Hospital.

unmarried women we find that girls begin masturbating at a much earlier period, many as early as five, although eight marks a distinct rise in the number, with the period of intense focus ranging from nine to twelve. This difference in ages is to be explained in large part, of course, on the basis of sex development occurring with greater rapidity in the girl than in the boy. That masturbation should be resorted to in such a sweeping and consuming manner and at such early ages is only another indictment of the moral attitude which prevents sex-instruction to the young as well as the old. It is this moral attitude with which we have been fettered for centuries, that increases sex-insanity within our midst while we dedicate our moral philippics to the perpetuation of purity.[6]

Among 1000 married women, we find the problem of masturbation again significant. It must be remembered that 68% of these women are college graduates and that their reaction, in one sense at least, is higher

[6] One of the most striking because most ridiculous recommendations in the cause of middle-class virtue is that made by W. F. Robie ("Rational Sex Ethics"). Mr. Robie, morbidly anxious to protect the purity of youth from the impurities of its recent revolt, idiotically suggests masturbation, which he euphemistically describes as "solitary sex relief," as a solution. It has been through such thoroughly warped suggestions and egregious stupidities made in defense of the old morals, that virtue has become vicious.

than that of girls less tutored and in positions of less
advantageous character. 381 of these married women
practice masturbation, and 183 have had "homosexual
relations with physical expression." 65 of them have
practiced both homosexuality and masturbation.[7] This
testimony is valuable from two points of view; first,
that it indicates something of the extensity of sex-
deviations among women who are married, and secondly, it illustrates the failure of marriage to supply
a satisfactory adjustment to the sex-impulse of many
women. As we indicated before, on the whole, sex-
relations should signify a cessation of masturbation,
unless the sex-relations are unfelicitous. A decrease
in masturbation on the part of unmarried and married
women, nevertheless, is to be noted. Dr. Davis' comparative reports reveal 60.3% of unmarried women
as indulging, or having indulged, in masturbation, and

[7] Masturbation and other erotic practices, among 1000 married
women, 68% of whom are college graduates.

Masturbation only	267
Sex intercourse only (before marriage)	20
Homosexual experience only (with physical expression)	83
Both masturbation and homosexual experience	65
Both masturbation and sexual intercourse	36
Both sexual intercourse and homosexual experience	2
Masturbation, sex intercourse, and homosexual experience	13
All these experiences denied	506
Questions relating to all these experiences	8
	1000

38.1% married. Those who had both masturbated and had homosexual experience among the unmarried totalled 787, or 78.7%; among the married they totalled 544, or 54.4%. This difference is not astonishing; it may even be called natural. What is arresting, however, is the degree of sex-deviations that are to be found even among women for whom marriage should have provided a normal erotic life. The bankruptcy and failure of marriage only receive further illustration from such investigations which penetrate into the secrets of sexual experience and response.

The maladjustments which marital existence has created, of course, betray themselves in neurosis and psychosis, and the overt insanities, as well as in such a perverted practice as masturbation or such a legal device as divorce.

The morality which has endeavored to force continence upon youth until its economic capacity can overtake its sexual has been one of the main contradictions at the root of this problem of masturbation. The revolt of youth in our generation, fortunately, has tended to encourage a laxity in sex relations that has been of particular advantage to the young who otherwise would have been crucified in the conflict between ethics and impulse. Youth is not to be intimidated by the silences that once awed and terrified its elders.

Sex is an important but not necessarily a secret and sacred thing.

Companionate marriage, therefore, has played an important rôle in bridging something of the huge gap between the early and rapid development of the sexual impulse and the late and delayed development of economic capacity, and thus will be able to save youth from many of the mental and physical lacerations which it has hitherto had to encounter in post-adolescent years. These lacerations in many cases have been extremely destructive; in most cases they have been severe. Contemporary youth, with its advocacy of necking and petting as part of normal behavior, and its willingness to contract companionate marriages in secret, has already achieved a partial emancipation. Lindsey wishes to save this emancipation from chaos. He fears promiscuity as its outcome. Legalized companionate marriage, therefore, is advised as a moral regulation. Those who have been so furious in their attacks upon its immoral character are already committed to the old forms, and cannot detect change until it overwhelms them. The desire to legalize companionate marriage is not the outgrowth of the feverish brain of an advanced judge. It is an outgrowth of the environment. It is only because we have such things as companionate marriages in private among the youth of today, that a man such as Judge Lindsey ventures the motion that they be legalized in order to avoid the dishonesty of the hypocrite and the secrecy of the sinner.

Companionate marriage, as a legislative enactment, is a direct *legal* stab at the old marital order, and the original concept of monogamous marriage. The existence of illegal companionate marriages had started to undermine the marital system long before the recent attempt to legalize the companionate marriage had ever begun. Legalized companionate marriage would only give lawful sanction to the process of disintegration. Bishop Fiske and Bishop Manning are correct in their statements that companionate marriage denies the fundamental proposition of the marital institution. The fundamental proposition of the marital institution of monogamy, which our social and economic order ordains, is that of permanency. Marriage entered into without the idea of permanence as its guiding motivation, may be called marriage still but it is not what the concept of monogamous marriage is supposed to convey. According to law and moral ideal, divorce should be sought only on the basis of extreme necessity, and even then hesitatingly and with utmost reluctance. Companionate marriage obscures the element of permanency and emphasizes the right of change and

[165]

choice. Young people are to marry companionately, which means with a full understanding that, if there are no children, separation is to be neither difficult nor delayed. It stresses the pragmatic aspect of heterosexual relationships, and not the metaphysical and mystical. It attempts to compromise with the sexual impulse, and not to deny and evade it.

The enthusiasm for companionate marriage is, after all is said, nothing more than another attestation of the failure of *uncompanionate* marriage.

CHAPTER VIII

PROSTITUTION AND THE NEW MORALS

ONE of the most interesting and striking effects of this new morality and the decay of marriage is the obvious decline which has occurred in prostitution. Perhaps it would be more precise to describe the change in terms of the fading appeal that the prostitute has come to have for modern youth. It is not that the economic situation which is the fundamental cause of prostitution has been altered, but that the necessity of the prostitute has diminished with the greater opportunity for sex relations upon the basis of mutual attraction. If the trade of the prostitute has not seriously decreased in connection with men of the old generation, it, nevertheless, has unquestionably declined with the youth of the new. Few men would ever choose the prostitute as a means of expressing their sexual urge if a less indelicate adjustment were attainable. The prostitute has been scorned by the very men who have turned to her for escape.

The story of prostitution is a story of bodies bartered for sustenance. While the history of prostitution had a picturesque career in the life of ancient as well as modern society, it was the Industrial Revolution that turned it from a practice into a plague. The terrific growth of prostitution in the last few centuries attests the evil effects of our economic system and the bankruptcy of the marital institution that has grown out of it. As Bernard de Mandeville so correctly observed many years ago the prostitute has been of great service to married men as well as unmarried. In reference to prostitution and its relationship to monogamous marriage, Mandeville's comment is signal. All men, asserts Mandeville, become physically tired of their wives and find the prostitute a very necessary and delectable variation. His own words are striking:

"A proof of this truth (that prostitution is a needed and valuable diversion) is the established maxim among women that the debauchees are mostly married men."

In another work of the same century (1727), "A Modest Defence of Public Stews" [1] the author fortifies the same contention by very extensive and detailed logic. He even outlines the number of lupinars and the section of London in which they should be situated, *in order to provide sufficiently for masculine impulse*

[1] Stew was an old English word used for brothel.

*and protect thereby, respectable girls and respectable
morality.*

In other words certain women have had to prostitute
themselves in order that other women might remain
respectable and that monogamous marriage continue
as a flexible fiction. Wherever sex desire was thwarted,
the prostitute offered a ready recourse. Cultured and
uncultured, men dedicated to professions sacred as
well as profane, have all found her an enticing diversion. Altogether prostitution is one of the boldest and
basest expressions of man's inhumanity to women. It
is the direct result of a morality made for men and
not for women.[2]

With the advancing independence of women and
their revolt against the old morality, and with the more
liberal outlook upon the sexual relation which has
grown out of this advance and revolt, and the decay

[2] That the problem of prostitution is fundamentally economic is
proven by an occupational study of the lives of those who have been
sucked into the vortices of its life. It is the proletariat which provides the greatest number of prostitutes. In Ryan's study of the
occupations of the majority of prostitutes he found that most came
from the following trades: milliners, dressmakers, straw bonnet makers,
furriers, hat binders, silk winders, tambour-workers, shoe-binders,
sales girls, and servants. Archenholtz and Rodenberg both report
that whole families at times are fed by prostitution. With the increase in the proletariat, an industrialism necessarily forces more and
more women into its ranks, the spread of prostitution has assumed
monstrous proportions. As an illustration of how rapidly the practice

of marriage as a sacred inspiration to rigid virtue, the prostitute is beginning to lose her monopoly upon the avenues of erotic escape. With youth this is particularly manifest. At one time the young man had practically no other retreat than that of the brothel. *Respectable* girls, in the old days, as we have seen, were taught to avoid even the minor intimacies of the kiss before betrothal. The passionate caress was a violation of respectable virtue. In these days of petting and

of prostitution has increased in the last hundred and fifty years, the conditions in England may be cited.

In 1777 there were			75,000	prostitutes in London		
In 1880	"	"	80,000	"	"	"
In 1820	"	"	100,000	"	"	"
In 1830	"	"	120,000	"	"	"
In 1840	"	"	160,000	"	"	"
In 1850	"	"	200,000	"	"	"
In 1860	"	"	228,000	"	"	"

It has been estimated by H. France that the increase since than has been at an average 20,000 to 40,000 every ten years, which means that in 1900 there were approximately 300,000 prostitutes in London. The statistical data gathered by Talbot and Ryan were somewhat lower but their figures were limited chiefly to police records and other very confined data.

As another evidence of the economic factor involved in the so-called moral attitude taken toward prostitution, an English law passed during the reign of Henry the Second is extremely informing: "No single woman to take money to lye with any man, except she lye with him all night, till the morrow." This ruling was ordained by the House of Commons and confirmed by the House of Lords and the King. It manifests the official attitude toward prostitution, with a clear recognition of obligations on the part of both employer and employe.

necking, however, and the freedoms that often follow, the difficulties incident to sex expression have largely disappeared.

"Necking in itself has already lowered—and if properly encouraged would still further decrease greatly—the amount of vice among college men. Under the present short-sighted rules, whether it has done the same for college women is doubtful. Twenty or thirty years ago, as some of the boys of that time tell us, it was quite regular and ordinary for a large number of college men to visit the 'tenderloin' districts, with, of course, terrible results. Some fraternities even maintained private institutions of this nature. That was in the pre-necking era. The cloistered students had no contact with decent women, and so they used such means as were at their disposal. But with the advent of the petting-party that has largely changed." [3]

In the instance of the questionnaire on morals at Amherst that we discussed in an earlier chapter it may be remembered that the majority of these men who had had sex relations did not have them in houses dedicated to amorous gratifications or with women active in such pursuits. Upon further questioning, each of the seven men who had had sexual intercourse admitted that part of his experience had been with girls and women who were totally alien to the profes-

[3] *New Student*—April 7, 1926.

sion of the prostitute. Of the six who had stated that they had visited a brothel, three declared that they had done so out of curiosity and had not copulated. In brief, prostitution has become much less popular among these college men, because, with the loosening of the old morals, sexual experience with women of the new generation is certainly to be preferred.

In the study made by Drs. Peck and Wells,[4] which we also cited in another reference in a previous chapter, the following question is immediately germane to our present consideration:

Question: *What proportion of your acts of sexual intercourse do you suppose to have been with prostitutes? (a prostitute, within the meaning of the question—is a woman who accepts these relations primarily on a commercial basis.)*

> *a.* None with prostitutes 21%
> *b.* About ¼% 4½%
> *c.* About ½% 3%
> *d.* About ¾% 2%
> *e.* All or practically all 4½%

What is at once significant is that 21% of these men did not have a single one of their sex relationships with prostitutes, and that only 4½% had all of their sex relationships with them. This is a further corro-

[4] "A Study in the Psycho-Sexuality of College Graduate Men."

boration of our contention. The young man of today
is turning away from the prostitute because he can
find his sex expression with the so-called "decent" girl
who has adopted the new morals. Only 14% of these
men had had any contact with the prostitute at all.
How important this is one can only realize when he
takes into consideration the fact that in the days before
the War, when the old morality was still in the stirrups,
at least 90% of these men would have had their sex-
relationships entirely with prostitutes. It has only
been with the rise of the new morality that this con-
tamination could be avoided.

What we discover in the decline of prostitution is a
realization of the important part that birth control has
played in the development of a finer expression of the
sexual impulse. While all of the factors which we
have considered in connection with the rise of the new
morality have been instrumental in bringing about this
freer expression of the sexual urge, it has been the invention of birth control methods which has made possible the "geologic shift in the center of gravity from
procreation to recreation as the true goal of sex expression." [5] The flapper and the new woman, informed

[5] "Is Prostitution Petering Out," Gilbert K. Shaw (Samuel D.
Schmalhausen)—*The Modern Quarterly,* November 1927-February
1928, Vol. 4, No. 3.

in the ways of enjoying sex as recreation without procreation, are freeing sex expression from its old fetters.
Their effect upon the decline of prostitution, however,
is scarcely more direct or definite than upon the general bankruptcy of marriage.

CHAPTER IX

ABORTION AND THE BANKRUPTCY OF THE OLD MORALS

IT is in the development of such phenomena as abortion and illegitimacy that we can observe the failure of the old moral order in obvious form and vivid array. This failure is directly connected with the failure of the marital institution, and the influence of marriage as an incentive to virtue. It is a failure that becomes increasingly tragic as we trace its manifestations in various phases of life. Here we have not intelligent revolt, but clandestine escape sought in ways at once barbarous and brutal. This escape is necessitated by the nature of the old morals. The old morals and the old marriage order enforced certain forms of behavior that often were in direct conflict with both economics and impulse, and which were bound to cause distress and disaster. The attitude toward abortion and birth control, for instance, was an absurd and dangerous contradiction. Abortion was condemned—and still is!—as a crime of grave consequence, but birth control, which in large part might prevent abortion, was also—and still is officially!—

condemned as an evil practice. The result has been that abortion has become a spreading menace.

In primitive times abortion was often resorted to without evasion. There were exceptions, it is true, and of such the instance of the ancient Maori is a singularly interesting illustration. The Maori condemned abortion but recommended the preventive methods of birth control.[1] Moreover, their attitude toward sex was of such a type as would justify the existence of such an ethic. It was the sacred duty of the men and women of the Maori to indulge in the sexual experience before marriage, and not to submit themselves to an enforced continence.[2] With many primitive peoples, however, abortion was a common and accepted practice.[3] In ancient times, Aristotle and Plato approved of it, and both Greek and Roman law, by denying consciousness and a soul to the embryo and the fœtus, gave it sanction. It was the Christian concept of the soul, and the necessity of baptism in order to insure resurrection after death, that altered this attitude. It was in A. D. 200, during the age of the Roman jurist

[1] "Social Hygiene of the New Zealand Maori," E. A. Rout; page 615. *Medical Journal and Record,* Vol. 124, 1926.

[2] A very advanced form of Companionate Marriage was practiced by them centuries ago, without disturbing the apparent serenity of their sexual relations.

[3] Sumner, "Folkways."

Ulpianus, that abortion was first condemned in the western world. The doctrine, which had declared the fœtus to be but part of the mother, and, therefore, without a soul of its own, was now outmoted by the baptismal theory of Christian dogma. Abortion became punishable by death. It was not until the eighteenth century that the severity of the penalty was somewhat mitigated.

It is not the purpose of this chapter to deal with the personal theory of abortion, which involves the right of the pregnant woman to decide whether she desires to have her child or not, save to say, as Havelock Ellis has pointed out in his excellent volume on "Sex in Relation to Society," that the present tendency among certain jurists, as well as the attitude of the populace as expressed in practice rather than theory, and the general direction in the changing attitudes toward sex, all favor the gradual return of this principle of personal privilege. No less distinguished a criminologist than Hans Gros has stated that very soon there will no longer be any punishment for abortion. Balestrini, Camilla Jellinek, Radbrush, Von Lilienthal, Jean Darricarrere, Kurt Hiller, and Elizabeth Zanzinger have uttered the same opinion.[4] In Germany the move-

[4] *Ibid.*

ment in favor of this attitude is very pronounced. At a woman's congress, in 1905, for example, a resolution was passed, which urged that abortion should not be punished except when the element of coercion was involved.[5]

Our problem is with abortion as it exists in our world today. First, it must be remembered, abortion in the modern world, with the exception of Soviet Russia, is illegal. The effect of this illegality in itself is enormous. It creates tendencies that are essentially destructive. It converts an evil into a cancer. It encourages subterfuge, hypocrisy, and crime. If the demand for abortions exists, and such a demand, as we indicated, is inevitable in modern society, then an intelligent tactic must be devised in order to meet or eliminate it. One thing is obvious at least from our past experience with criminality, and that is that to declare an act as crime is not preventing its expression. The truth of this has been revealed by our own experience with prohibition. Only education, that grows out of an improving economic and social environment, and works a change upon attitudes, can effect an alteration in behavior that cannot be achieved by legal astringency or punitive threat. The desire for abortion arises out of the desire of a woman to avoid having a child

[5] *Ibid.*

because the child may represent an inconvenience, it may bring on disgrace, it may threaten her physical well-being, handicap her work, hinder her freedom. These, and many other reasons, may be conspicuous as the actual cause. The causes may vary in importance and gravity. In a large percentage of instances the need for abortion arises directly out of the factors of economics and ignorance. The mother cannot afford another child; the presence of other children, conditions of deprivation, or the elements of disease or incapacitation on the part of the husband, may be the cause. In many of such cases, which are appallingly frequent among the proletariat, conception can be attributed more often to ignorance of application rather than ignorance of the existence of birth control methods. It is our contention that there are comparatively few people who are unaware of the existence of methods of birth control. As we have pointed out, however, two factors intervene and prevent their application: that of economics, which makes the most popular and perhaps the only contraceptive known to many people utterly beyond their reach save as an occasional luxury; and that of ignorance of application which results in people's using contraceptive methods without sufficient scientific knowledge of their means of effective manipulation and control. If scientific application of birth control technique were taught, such calamities, in most part, could certainly be avoided.

In many other cases, the desire for abortion has an entirely *moral* motivation. The unmarried girl deserted by her lover is the case featured by the novelist and playwright, and is too well-known to the public to need discussion. Hundreds of thousands of such girls each year help support the trade of the professional "abortionist." Harried by moral fears and the dread of social obloquy, and often its ensuing economic handicap and loss, they are in fit mood to be exploited by the extortionate demands of the abortionist. Many of these girls who retreat to the abortionist, might hazard the economic handicap of the child, if the moral stigma were not so drastic and profound. Many of them indeed might even want the child, in fact would seek and not avoid the experience of motherhood, if there were no moral penalty to undergo. It can easily be seen, then, that if our code of morals did not exclude the unmarried mother and classify her as an outcast, many abortions would never occur. In illustration of the prevalence of abortion among the unmarried, evoked as such cases are in the main by moral fear, certain statistics gathered in Hamburg are of interest. Among 31 cases of criminal abortion that were studied, the ages of the women ranging from eighteen to twenty-

four, 29 were unmarried and only two were married.[6]
As the ages increase, in correspondence with the rising
ratio of marriage, the tendency of abortions among
married women, of course, becomes more frequent than
among single. That between the ages of 18-24 the
disparity should be so great, in favor of the unmarried
however, is a fact of not a little importance. It indicates the direction of moral trends, the dangerous
influence of an old morality that cannot adapt itself
to the new ideals and shibboleths.

The suppression of all instruction in birth-control
technique and the condemnation of all children born
out of wedlock are at the basis of the abortion-evil.
Such has been the cost of the old morality!

That all other causes of abortion are subordinate to
the two which we have just noted in some detail is
obvious without argument. The women who desire
abortions because the prospect of a child may interfere
with the freedom of their lives, the convenience of unhampered contacts, the achievements of a career, are,
after all, not nearly so numerous in comparison. Nor
are the number of women who desire abortions because
of physical illness as great as those falling to the first
two groups. Dr. Edward A. Schumann, writing on the

---

[6] "Beitrag zur Statistik krimineller Aborte," Dr. Arthur Horvat in
Monatsschrift für Geburtshilfe und Gynäkologie. Pp. 278-283. 1922.

"Economic Aspects of Abortion," [7] states, for instance, that "from 80% to 85% of all cases of induced abortion occur among married women who have had one or more children, and were at the time of the abortion living with their husbands." Although such a figure could scarcely be verified upon a large scale, and while the percentage of married women, upon further analysis, might be found to be somewhat exaggerated, the evidence it attests is at once enlightening and important. The existence of these abortions, it is clear, was due either to errors in the application of birth-control technique or in entire ignorance of it. It is not overstatement to say that 99% of these women would have preferred the methods of contraception to those of abortion. How eager these women would have been to secure more scientific knowledge of contraception is evinced by the attitudes of the English women who applied for assistance at the Mother's Clinic of Dr. Marie Stopes in England. Among the 5000 cases treated during the first 3½ years that the clinic was in operation, 4,834 women sought counsel as to contraception. Dr. Schumann, in the above paper, it should be added, looks to the control of conception as the most promising means of meeting the increasing menace

[7] Abstract of a paper presented at the meeting of the Obstetrical Society of Philadelphia. October 12, 1923.

of abortion. It is not a surprise, therefore, to observe Margaret Sanger describing this situation as "a disgrace to civilization," and attributing it to the "puritanical blindness (which) insists upon suffering and death from ignorance rather than life and happiness through knowledge and prevention."

Commenting upon the criminal abortionist, Dr. Howard Kelly admitted a certain fact that is, in a way, an attestation of the nature of public sentiment.

"The punishment of such criminals (criminal abortionists) is always difficult," wrote Dr. Kelly, "as popular sympathy is rather with the abortionist and murdered, and the witness is apt to be an unwilling one." [8]

If the popular sympathy is with the abortionist, as Dr. Kelly states, and as in so many cases is revealed, then it seems obvious that the attitude toward abortion is one which is friendly rather than hostile. Of course, the great number of women who have to resort to it, the difficulties that it can save or conceal, all tend to incline many to accept it as a necessary and at times fortunate operation. Certainly women, particularly those that are married, unless intimidated by a religious superstition, attach no particular stigma to it. Without question, they will admit unhesitatingly often

[8] *Medical Gynecology.*

the fact of an abortion they had undergone, while they would carefully conceal the existence of any extra-marital relationship. This attitude must be taken into consideration when we study the statistics of abortions that confront us.

The prevalence of abortion throughout the western world is made all the more terrifying by the numerous fatalities that are incurred. That these fatalities are not due to the gravity of the operation, but to the fact that the operation usually must be undertaken in a clandestine manner without the advantages of a sanitary technique, will be admitted by practically every unprejudiced obstetrician. Furthermore, the charlatans to whom women are often forced to turn for the operation are both ill-equipped and unskilled craftsmen. Their knowledge of the sterilization of instruments, and the means of preventing septicemia, is frightfully limited. Yet it is these charlatans who constitute the larger percentage of abortionists in the western world. As an instance of the effectiveness of scientific technique and unscientific manipulation—a contrast which we shall deal with more fully in a later chapter—Soviet Russia reports that in 55,320 legal abortions that were effected in 1922, 1923, and 1924, there was not a single mortality, but in 66,675 cases effected by illegal practices, 3000 fatalities resulted.[9] This is an astonishing and significant contrast. Its meaning is profound.

Let us observe something of the spread of abortion in the western world. In Venice criminal abortions have been five times more frequent since the War. In Austria the increase has been so alarming that there is a demand for the enactment of a new law to meet the situation.[10] The increase in abortions in Germany has been pronounced. Between 1880 and 1890 there were only nine or ten miscarriages to 100 pregnancies, at present there are 15 to 20; in some regions almost 40. According to Freudenberg, during 1909-21, from 10% to 40% of the pregnancies of Berlin were terminated by abortion, while similar statistics are reported from other cities. Professor Bumm reported that, according to statistics collected by the University Woman's Clinic, between 1860 and 1880, 10.6% of the pregnancies were terminated by abortion; from 1890 to 1900 it rose to 19%, and during the first decade of this century, to 24%. Of 100 women who, in 1916, within four weeks, presented themselves at the clinic on account of incomplete abortion, 89 had used

[9] *Journal of American Medical Association*—"Gynecology and Foreign Governments"; by Holden. Page 2014.
[10] *Ibid.*

artificial means.[11] The following table which shows the ratio between abortions and births in Mainz (1910-20) is of unusual value in revealing the steady increase that is to be noted from 10.20% in 1910 to 26.03% in 1920.[12]

TABLE

Year	Ratio in Percentage
1910	10.20
1911	13.93
1912	14.58
1913	17.23
1914	17.88
1915	18.04
1916	15.90
1917	24.64
1918	26.86
1919	23.00
1920	26.03

In America the condition is even more deplorable. While Paris is well known for its abortions, there are not a few American cities that are its serious rival. Lewin states that in New York City, 80,000 criminal abortions are performed every year. The death-rate from these abortions has been estimated at 33⅓%.[13]

[11] *Journal of American Medical Association*—Vol. 88. No. 4. Page 259.

[12] *Zentralblatt fur Gynakologie*. Nov. 19, 1921.

Philbrick, citing the Committee appointed by the Michigan Board of Health in 1881, maintains that ⅓ of all pregnancies terminate in criminal abortions, that 100,000 criminal abortions occur in the United States every year, and that at least 6,000 women die of the consequences of the operation.[14] Tobinson in 1919 estimated that there are 1,000,000 criminal abortions effected each year in the United States. In terms of birth-ratios, that means since there are approximately 2,400,000 children born each year, that there is one criminal abortion for every two and one-half births.[15] In this same study, it is estimated that 8,000 deaths occur as a result of criminal abortion in New York City alone each year, and that the total for the country must reach 50,000.

The disparities in these estimates are not unexpected, since the very illegality of the operation prevents statistical exactitude, and all calculations must be made from limited observations and scattered materials. Nevertheless, what definite data we do possess leads us to infer that the latter estimates of Tobinson are closer to reality than those of Lewin and Philbrick. For instance, out of Hellier's series of 1,000 married women,

[23] "The Legalization of Abortion," Morris H. Kahn; *American Medicine*. March 1927.

[14] *Ibid.*

[25] The Frequency and Cause of Abortion," Arthur Wm. Meyer.

of proletarian background, 89.2 had one or more abortions.[16]   In the Carnegie cases examined, 92.2% had abortions, many repeated abortions, although only 5.6% had aborted more than five times.[17]   Of 697 women studied at the Carnegie Laboratories there were 1,351 children 1,843 abortions—1.3 abortions for every birth. Of course, in all such calculations the fact that perhaps as many as one-third of the abortions which actually occur are not induced but spontaneous must be taken into consideration. Of those abortions resulting from purely maternal, paternal, or fœtal factors, syphilis is the most frequent cause. In 657 syphilitic women there were, for example, 35% of abortions.[18]   Of course, in the large estimates that we have cited, it is induced abortions that are stressed. Furthermore, the tendency to conceal an induced abortion beneath the cloak of the fortuitous tends to ostensibly lessen the actual number of cases of voluntary abortions. Dr. Wright, with caution that is very marked, estimates, that for every one abortion that is spontaneous, two are induced.[19]   In a study of 164 selected women, there were found that among the 664 pregnancies recorded, there were 348 which terminated

[16] *Ibid.*   [17] *Ibid.*

[18] J. E. Davis, *Journal of Michigan State Medical Society,* 1918.

[19] Dr. A. H. Wright, Toronto.   Cf. Sajou's "Analytic Cyclopoedia of Practical Medicine."

in abortion. 51 of the 164 women confessed to their having had induced abortions, some of them repeatedly. These 51 women had 220 pregnancies, of which 118 resulted in abortion. Of these, 71.1% were induced.[20] The figures collected by G. Rimette at the Paris Maternité, from 1897 to 1905, are also of value. Among 9,875 pregnancies there were 1,457 induced abortions, 367 infected abortions and 627 spontaneous abortions. 27 deaths resulted from them all. Among the 464 women that were studied at a Municipal Birth Control Clinic, M. H. Kahn observed that 192 had had abortions or miscarriages, that a number of these women had had them several times, totalling 324 pregnancies which they had interrupted.[21] In another instance of 113 cases of maternal mortality that were studied by the state department of health in Michigan, abortion was found to be the direct or contributory cause in at least 35 cases, and of the 47 cases of septicemia, 28 followed abortions.[22] Even among the married women whom we cited in one of the studies of Dr. K. B. Davis the percentage of abortions was exceptionally numerous. Until the moral code and social attitude which outlaws the unmarried mother,

[20] Royston, *American Journal of Obstetrics*, Oct. 1917.
[21] *N. Y. Medical Journal*, 1917.
[22] *Journal of American Medical Association*, page 1158. 1927.

and the statutory provision which prevents instruction in the scientific methods of birth-control, are changed or disappear, the practice of abortion cannot be curbed. With the young generation and the new morality, as we already know, this moral code and social attitude are already in a process of change and disintegration. With the young generation, too, knowledge of contraceptives is also far more widespread, although this knowledge in many instances is still far from scientific. As an immediate palliative, however, only scientific instruction in the use of contraceptives, is of practical value. Dr. M. H. Kahn, to whom we referred in an earlier paragraph in this chapter, has made it unmistakably clear that to limit abortion we must learn to prevent undesired conceptions. Dr. Kahn has gathered some convincing statistics in connection with this contention. Among the 464 women cited above, 272 were aware of birth-control methods, and 192 were not. Among the 272 women there were only 72 who had undergone abortions, with a total of 122 abortions; among the 192 there were 104 who had had abortions, with a total of 202 abortions. This contrast furnishes a hopeful indication of the extent to which abortions may be diminished when the methods of contraception become more widely known and understood.

The methods that are used in America today to combat abortions are superficial and ineffective. They are grounded on ignorance and superstition. They continue a tradition that has long outworn its use. Legal decrees cannot suppress what the populace desires and demands. But legal decrees can create a thriving illegal trade or profession—which they often have. And the costs of these illegal trades, are often very terrible, indeed. In the matter of abortions, the economic factor is an important determinant. The proletariat pays the price of poverty. It must turn to the quack and charlatan for its aid, not to the high-priced professional who serves the needs of the wealthier classes. Subsequent disease and very often death are far more frequent with the first group than the second. So long as abortion remains an illegal operation, the poor will inevitably suffer more than the rich. Only with abortion legalized as in Soviet Russia, with the privilege open to all classes without charge, can this class discrimination be prevented. It is in the direction of the elimination of abortion however that we must labor. This can be done only by educating people in the science of birth control, and changing their economic life, so that coming of children is no longer a burden.

The new morality is dedicated to the former end; the new economic society must be dedicated to the latter.

CHAPTER X

ILLEGITIMACY AND REVOLT

I N the growth of illegitimacy we are confronted with certain of the more unfortunate aspects of the changing morals. As Lindsey has informed us from the cases in his court, the number of young girls who become pregnant as a consequence of the new freedom in sex relations that prevail among modern youth has steadily increased in recent years. This is to be expected as long as birth control methods are not divulged in the form of scientific instruction. With college youth the catastrophes on the whole are no doubt less numerous than among the less tutored classes. Col. Margaret Bovil of the Salvation Army, for instance, reports that:

"Forty-two per cent of unmarried mothers cared for in the last two years in 15 Salvation Army Homes in the eastern territory were school girls of an average age of sixteen. . . .

"In spite of reforms such as doing away with red light districts, the Salvation Army has in this territory twice the

number of maternity homes it operated in these lurid days
of the past and they are filled to capacity—by whom? Not
by professionals, but by school children, many of whom
have been obliged to leave their desks in high or elementary
grades to go direct to our institutions. . . .

"The cities covered in the survey and the percentage of
girls whose age averages sixteen in the Salvation Army maternity home of each of these cities follows:

"Philadelphia, 75%; Jersey City, 60%; Pittsburgh,
50%; Buffalo, 40%; Cincinnati (white), 70%; Cincinnati
(Negro), 60%; Birmingham, 25%; Boston, 13%; Cleveland (white), 22%; Cleveland (Negro), 60%; Louisville,
20%; Roanoke, 50%; Wilmington, 35%; New York City,
20%; Richmond, 40%."

Of course, statistics on illegitimacy indicate but a
limited phase of the change, since more pregnancies
are unquestionably terminated by abortions than are
allowed to attain expression in birth. Last year there
were 57,851 illegitimate children whose births were
recorded in the United States census,[1] and from these
statistics as a whole we find that the larger part of

---

[1] This figure, unfortunately, is not precise, for several reasons that
we shall enumerate. First, many states fail to compile separate statistics for illegitimacy, and, therefore, their totals cannot be included
in the above figure. Secondly, many illegitimate births are not registered at all, and hence cannot be included in this total. Thirdly,
incorrect information entered on the birth certificate often happily
conceals an illegitimacy beneath the shield of legitimacy. The total,
therefore, is one that suffers from understatement and not exaggeration.

unmarried mothers are girls in their teens. More than one-sixth of unmarried mothers are girls under eighteen years of age. A striking comparison, for instance, is to be found, in the case of first births, in the number of unmarried mothers and the number of married. Between the ages of 18 to 20, for instance, the proportion of unmarried mothers is 3% higher than married. Among those between 21 and 24, the same proportion exists. Above that age, as would be expected, the proportions are reversed. In Boston 43% of the unmarried mothers in one year were under 21 years of age, and 13% under 18 years of age. Among the fathers 21% were less than 21 years of age, and 4% less than 18. As an instance also of the prevalence of extra-marital relations, and of the failure of marriage to attain monogamous fidelity, among the cases of illegitimacy reported by Boston agencies, 21% of the fathers were married to other women. In these cases also youth was not inconspicuous.

That one in every twenty-three births in Boston is illegitimate, that 2,108 illegitimate children were born in that city in the year 1914; [2] that in Baltimore there are 24 agencies actively at work with the problem of illegitimacy; that 22 babies were advertised for adop-

---

[2] "Illegitimacy as a Child Welfare Problem," Part II. (U. S. Dept. of Labor.)

tion in one month in St. Louis by a maternity home; that more than 1,000 infants are lost every year in Chicago without the slightest record of their destiny; [3] that baby farms exist where infants are often sent to die; that traffic in illegitimate children through advertisement and assignation is a thriving trade—that such things exist is sufficient testimony in itself of the injurious consequences of trying to enforce an antiquated and unnatural ethic.[4]

In these conditions we detect not only the disinte-

[3] Mangold, "Reports of Boards of Charity of Indiana."

[4] The actual toll that is exacted by this ethic in terms of life and death, individual and social suffering, is seldom realized and understood. A morality that could build up a prejudice against a child. because its parents are unmarried is founded on cruelty and ignorance, with almost an element of the fiendish in its aspect; it expresses the dominance of the property-concept over the personal. The unmarried mother is forced to all manner of extremities of concealment and expenditure in order to give birth to her child. The moral scorn which she encounters certainly does not strengthen her mental equilibrium. Her nervous system is often shaken and shattered by this phase of the experience alone. In homes of confinement where many girls have to retreat, she is always aware of her position as an unfortunate and delinquent. In such homes her care is never of the kind which would encourage an attitude or outlook of a salutary character. Her daily diet is in the form of admonition and sermon. She is taught to look upon herself as not very dissimilar from a criminal. In the world at large, her plight is even worse. In addition to the moral stupidities of spinsters and the invidious disdain of married wives and mothers, she is confronted with an economic problem that in itself is often sufficient to make her courage crumble and weaken. As a consequence of all these factors, it is not only the mother who suffers but also the child. In the matter of still-births

grative forces active in moral decay, but, in addition, are brought to realize, when confronted by our earlier

the costs of this morality become unmistakably evident and glaring. The following table illustrates these costs in statistical form:

STILL BIRTHS PER 100 BIRTHS

Total for Birth Registration Area	*Legitimate*	*Illegitimate*
	3.9	8.8
White	3.5	6.7
Colored	7.4	11.2
Delaware	4.0	14.0
District of Columbia	4.5	9.9
Kentucky	3.2	10.0
Maryland	6.6	15.1
Mississippi	4.9	10.0
New Jersey	4.0	11.9

What we see from this table is that in every state there is a wide disparity between the number of still-births of married mothers and unmarried. In Norway between 1891 and 1900 still-births among illegitimate children were 164 to 165 compared with 100 still-births among legitimate children. That the mothers of illegitimate children are, on the whole, less healthy than those of legitimate is an unarguable proposition. In certain cases, it may be true, the parents of illegitimate children are sickly and diseased. But this is also true of married couples. The conservative will maintain that the larger number of still-births among unmarried than married mothers is due to syphilis. Even if we grant this to be true in a certain percentage of cases, allowing possibly, for the same argument, a small disparity as due to this factor, the fact still remains that, as a general, or even as the chief, explanation, this proposition is patently untenable and absurd. Syphilis is prevalent among the married as well as the unmarried. "Excluding the abandoned or vicious classes," writes Kelly in "Medical Gynecology," "practically all women who acquire material, their immediate influence upon youth. The seriousness of the problem of illegitimacy among youths

syphilis receive the infection from their husbands." While this observation may lack something of final cogency, it indicates at least the prevalence of venereal infections among the married. In a study of the origins of venereal infections, it was found in Berlin that, among other factors several thousand soldiers received only 30% of their infections from prostitutes and 21% from married women, widows and fiancées. (Hugo Hecht, *Mitt. de. Deutsch Gesellsch.*) It is increasingly obvious, then, that these disparities among the number of still-born children are to be attributed, in the main, to the morality which directly or indirectly handicaps and harms the pregnant woman who is unmarried.

If we examine the mortality of children born of illegitimate and legitimate parents, which is germane to the same problem, we shall discover that wherever these statistics are collected the mortality-rate of illegitimate children exceeds that of legitimate. The following table will illustrate the appalling differences in death-rate of the two groups:

MORTALITY OF ILLEGITIMATE INFANTS (1915) COMPARED WITH LEGITIMATE

Disease	*Proportion of Illegitimate to 100 Legitimate*	
	Males	Females
Atrophy, debility, etc.	284	252
Premature Birth	174	168
Whooping Cough	115	85
Diarrhea and Enteritis	226	232
Tuberculosic Disease	174	181
Syphilis	652	939
All Diseases	190	197

Is it not pertinent to ask, by way of consistence, are these illegitimate children unhuman, and undeserving of social consideration? Is the attitude which opposes abortion because it is a cruel violation of as well as adults, of course, is lessened somewhat by the easy access of the abortionist and the rapid dis-

the rights of existence in consonance with the one that discriminates against the child born of an unmarried mother? It can surely be said, without question, that the increased mortality or at least the major share of it in the case of illegitimate children is a consequence of an ethic which degrades and weakens the mother, and thwarts the life and growth of the child. The very fact of its unfailing occurrence, wherever this morality is dominant, is further evidence of the nature of its drastic influence. In Germany, for instance, in the one year, 1912, there were 183,857 illegitimate children born, 41,027 of which died under one year of age. The mortality rate for that year for these illegitimate children was 22%; for legitimate children it was only 14.7%. In the table appended immediately below, a picture of these differences in terms of English life is disclosed.

AVERAGE INFANT MORTALITY RATES FOR LEGITIMATE AND ILLEGITIMATE BIRTHS IN URBAN AND RURAL DISTRICTS OF ENGLAND AND WALES, 1912 TO 1917

Annual Number of Deaths under 1 year per 1000 Live Births					
	1912-1914			1915-1917	
			Relative			Relative
	Illegiti-mate	Legiti-mate	differ-ence	Illegiti-mate	Legiti-mate	differ-ence
England and Wales	200.4	98.3	2.0	195.8	94.1	2.1
Urban Districts	214.5	102.3	2.1	208.6	97.8	2.1
London	235.9	95.0	2.5	256.0	94.4	2.7
County Boroughs	231.0	112.6	2.1	218.2	106.2	2.1
% Other Urban districts	190.6	94.6	2.0	182.0	90.4	2.0
Rural Districts	149.6	81.5	1.8	148.2	78.9	1.9

In Denmark 213 illegitimate children die to every 100 legitimate; in Norway, 199 to 100; and Sweden, 178 to 100. In Italy where there have been over 150,000 illegitimate births in the three years of 1922 semination, in bootleg fashion, of knowledge of the devices of contraception. The number of abortions effected among girls under 21, it can be said from those observations which are sufficiently calculable, have certainly doubled if not tripled since the War. This increase, to be sure, was to be expected. The trade of the abortionist had begun to flourish, it must be remembered, during the period of the War, and this advance which has followed is but a continuation of a rising cause and effect sequence.

Another reflection of interest to our general analysis is the decisive influence of the economic factor in the problem. In the vast majority of cases we find that unmarried mothers are girls who are economically employed. They are girls who were engaged in either skilled or unskilled occupations, and not of the parasitic type that depend upon prostitution as a source of livelihood.

Eighty-six per cent of the unmarried mothers in Boston, to illustrate, are gainfully occupied. Of the girls between 16 and 20 years of age, 83% earn their own sustenance. Of those in the same group in the general population, it is interesting to note, only 60% are economically engaged. This correlation indicates the

(50,843), 1923 (49,272), and 1924 (53,874)—or one for each 21 legitimate births—the condition is similar.

tendency to freer expression of the sexual impulse on the part of those girls and women who are economically independent, or at least who are working for such independence, than on the part of those who are not. In all likelihood, this correlation will be found wherever women are active in economic life of the group.[5]

[5] Another phase of the economic element in the problem is to be discovered in the class-factor. The proletariat provides the larger number of illegitimate children. First, to be sure, there is the matter of numbers; the proletariat outnumbers the other classes in society. Secondly, the decay of the old family naturally began with the proletariat long before it began with the bourgeoisie. The Industrial Revolution, as we have shown, turned the family of the poorer classes into a cesspool of sickness and suffering. Its influence was immediately centrifugal. It shattered the old relations and the old ethics. Its destruction of the family as a unifying factor in social and moral life followed from the very nature of the new order. What has happened today is the accumulation of these influences, the extension of the tentacles of the industrial system which has brought the inclusion of other classes within their jaws, the proletarianization of larger and larger sections of the community, and the disintegration of the entire structure of the old family and home. The proletariat naturally shows the wider ravages of this change. It has suffered longer; its tendencies have become more sharpened; its ignorance has left it less protected. There are other conditioning factors, of course, which make illegitimacy a more obvious problem with the proletariat than with the upper classes. Birth control devices, for instance, can be purchased less readily and less frequently, and, on the whole, perhaps, can be managed with less success, by the proletariat than by the wealthier and less impoverished strata of the population. The unwanted illegitimate child, therefore, will be a more frequent result with this group than with others. Abortions also explain part of the discrepancy. The proletariat cannot resort to the abortionist with the same ease that the upper classes can, although the lower quacks and charlatans undoubtedly offer a medium to which the under-

It is only with the new morality and its disdain for the old stigmas that the attitude toward illegitimacy has begun to alter. In places we find the legal distinctions between the legitimate and the illegitimate child already removed. France has just recently destroyed the legal discrimination in favor of the legitimate child. The stand taken by the state of North Dakota in this country is of significance in this progress toward a more enlightened ethic. This state has declared that *every* child is the "legitimate" child of its natural parents, and, therefore, has eliminated any distinctions between children born in or out of wedlock. The child inherits from both parents and their relatives. The only necessity is that the mother establish paternity within a year after the child's birth. Other states have evinced a certain liberalism in their recent legislation in reference to illegitimacy and the unmarried mother. In Nevada, the illegitimate child is entitled to benefit under the Workmen's Compensation Act; Michigan and Nebraska have made provision for the unmarried mother. The Scandinavian countries

classes can and do turn in such an emergency. Perhaps, if totals could be calculated, it would be found that there is not such a wide gap here as at first might be suspected. Of course, even the lower charlatans demand a fee that very often neither the poor girl nor her family can afford, and this in itself would often necessitate the child instead of an artificially terminated pregnancy.

provide an additional illustration of a more advanced outlook upon this question.[6]

[6] In order to cope with the problem of illegitimacy, the creation of maternity houses has become a necessity. In two states, to illustrate, Minnesota and Pennsylvania, a study of thirty-five maternity homes, eleven in Minnesota and twenty-four in Pennsylvania, has already been prosecuted. In addition to these 35 maternity homes, the report ("A Study of Maternity Homes in Minnesota and Pennsylvania"—U. S. Dept. of Labor Children's Bureau Publications) states that there were numerous other homes indirectly connected with this work. The thirty-five studied fitted more precisely within the boundaries and aims of this study. In Minnesota, during the one year of 1922, in these homes and hospitals directly connected with them, there occurred 1151 live births, 29 still births, and 2 maternal deaths. In Pennsylvania during 1922, in 22 homes there were 1573 expectant mothers; 1492 live births occurred, 35 still births and 4 maternal deaths. While a few cases in both states were those of married women, the overwhelming majority, of course, were unmarried. In addition to these homes, as this report suggests, to be sure, there are in these states, and in every other state, many homes of similar character, operating under special disguise, that are never located. These homes vary according to the class of girl they endeavor to attract. There must be thousands of such homes scattered over the country; many of them are isolated in the outskirts of the suburban sections of a city, or often sequestered in an obscure town or hamlet.

One of the most interesting and best known homes of this type is The Veil which is located in Langhorne, Pa. This institution, since its inception, twenty years ago, has handled over 4000 cases, which means that each year it has undertaken the seclusion of approximately 200 girls—in 1923 it had 264 girls within its shelter. The girls cared for by this home are "not the immoral and degenerate type," writes one of its officials in a letter to a doctor "but worthy young women who wish to rectify their mistake, without disgrace to themselves or their families." The catalogue which this home, or Maternity Hospital, publishes, is very inviting and attractive. It certainly understands the importance of sanitary technique. By means of good literature, Bible instruction, and general supervision, it aims to prepare

In Germany, however, a more modern and revolutionary attitude toward the whole problem developed early in the twentieth century. The bankruptcy of marriage in Germany, for instance, is attested by the growth of illegitimacy in both city and province. For a period of over thirty years the illegitimate child has steadily undermined the marital institution. One out of every twelve babies born in Germany, for example, is illegitimate. In 1914 there were one million illegitimate children under fourteen years of age in Germany.[7] The right of the woman to have a child

its inmates for a high, ethical life after their departures from the institution. The children will be taken care of by the institution, and later adopted, if the mother wishes to be relieved of the child after its birth. In other words, everything is done to protect the mother from the condemnation of society by the introduction of such means of escape and seclusion. The girl can go to Europe for a period, she can visit a relative in New York, she can accept a position in Philadelphia, or go on an archeological expedition to Madagascar.

The existence of numerous retreats of this kind, in every section of the country, save our romantic idealists from an insight into the extensity of the moral problem. What occurs that cannot be seen does not perturb the souls of those enslaved by an archaic convention and custom. In this contradiction resides the essential *immorality* of the old morals.

Moreover, it must not be forgotten, such homes as The Veil, by the very nature of their fee, are organized for the middle classes. The upper classes, it might be said, seldom need to accept the aid of such retreats. Abortion is simpler. (And so often it is also with the proletariat—but what a contrast in the kind of abortion!) or a real trip to Paris is more convenient.

[7] Katharine Anthony, "Feminism in Germany and Scandinavia."

regardless of her unmarried state has been part of the cry that has now risen into a feminine challenge.

The recent *eugenic* baby, of course, is but one minor expression of this changing attitude in active form in the United States. Dora Russell's advocacy of a Trade Union for Women is in line with the same feminine logic of insurrection. In the Mutterschutz movement in Germany, however, the most daring proposal was made. This movement, which was founded in Berlin as early as 1905, with such distinguished figures as Ellen Key, Lily Braun, Marie Lichneuska and Adele Schreiber as its leaders, and Forel and Freud as its advocates, aimed at a general reformation of sexual ethics. It criticized the eternal validity of monogamy, and dedicated itself to the protection of motherhood as its fundamental purpose. Sensitive to the cruelties achieved by the morality which smiled upon the married mother and frowned upon the unmarried, and cognizant of the subordination of woman by man as the basic motivation of this ethic, it allied itself with an idealism that scorned such discriminations and inequalities. Woman must be freed of this fetter. She must escape the enslavements of such a barbarous morality by rising in revolt against it. There must be no distinction among mothers. All mothers are devoted to the same sacred cause of creation, married or unmarried.

Motherhood must be elevated beyond the qualifying categories of good and evil. It is a sacred function, which no woman should deny herself because of convention or custom. In order to shatter the existing distinctions which favored the married mother and condemned the unmarried, these idealists suggested a radical procedure:

"There is one radical method which would bring our ideas back upon the right track and many a sincere friend of the cause must have already wished it—that illegitimate births might occur with great frequency. For rights and laws, as they are, were not revealed by an unalterable cosmic order but framed by the temporary majority. And the majority is always right—even when it is wrong! Every century has a different law and one need not be a Utopian to assume that, after so and so many decades or centuries, the idea of illegitimate motherhood hitherto uncultivated may be transformed into its exact opposite. The more illegitimate births there are to record, the nearer comes the time. This would remind the prophets in the wilderness that their morality will appear tomorrow to their children's children as an absurdity. The young succeeds the old—the old morality gives way to the new."

With the dissolution of marriage as a sacred institution, and the growth of a new attitude toward sex as procreation as well as recreation, the stigma attached to the illegitimate mother and the illegitimate child has already begun to lose its force and influence. The changing mores are in conspiracy against it. It can only be with a new economic order, however, with the entire elimination of the property-element from the organization of sex life, that the final scars will disappear.

CHAPTER XI

THE NEW MORALITY IN GERMANY

BEFORE passing to Soviet Russia where we shall discover the old morality outworn and effete, and a new morality already in the process of social formulation, it is necessary for us to observe the changes that have occurred in ethical attitude in modern Germany where the transition from the old morality to the new has advanced with rapid strides. Germany may be said to represent this transition in its most interesting form. In Soviet Russia where the new moral attitude has state sanction, the chaos of transition is more individual than social. In Germany the chaos is social as well as individual. Nevertheless, out of this chaos German youth has striven to fuse a certain idealism into its insurrection. It has attempted to face its own actions with candour, criticizing excess, and yet not fearing to announce the extremities of its own challenge. This is more than can be said of the revolt of youth in America. In Russia, of course, this revolt is but part of an entire revolt against the old order, but one element in a manifold revolutionary synthesis, and youth has no need to declare what is already accepted, or announce what is commonly practiced.

In Germany, as in other countries, the changes in economic and social life, the decay of religion, the dissolution of the marital bond, and the new attitude of woman, have accomplished a vivid transformation in moral outlook. With the decline of religion as an ideal, those moral fears which it has foisted upon civilization have weakened if not disappeared. Youth has now informed the world that the threat of eternal damnation is no longer as strong as the inveigling appeal of momentary ecstasy.

"If marriage were not made by God, and torment in hell is probably not the result of adultery, there is no longer reason to think that five minutes' bliss must be paid for in terms of eternal damnation. It is, no doubt, true that God still loves the pure, but when earthly loves are available, the price of God's love may not be worth the paying."

In these words of C. E. M. Joad [1] we find this attitude tersely and wittily phrased. The thunderous wrath of the God of Endicott and Edwards no longer terrifies the youth of today who has made a kind of compromising peace with gods closer to the desires of his body and the tendencies of his era. In Soviet Russia the

[1] "Thrasymachus," C. E. M. Joad.

youth is educated in the virtue of atheism. In Germany the youth movement has turned from the old creeds.[2] Confirmation rites are now related frequently to their primitive origins in phallic worship and priapian ceremonies, with the atheist and free-thinker conspicuous often as orator and inspiration. Sexual interests have escaped indeed from their old incarceration.

In the German youth movement this escape has been attained in remarkably interesting and enlightened ways. Few movements in modern life will prove of such momentous consequence to future generations. A sense of solidarity akin almost to collectivization of impulse and decision has been able to develop that is of significance in the scale of moral and social relationships. New ways of thinking and acting have thus been able to escape the isolation of individual recommendation and achieve something of a social sweep and status. It is astonishing how widespread has been this change. German youth, like the youth in Russia, has now largely come to "discuss sex relations, abortions, and love with the candour of obstetricians."

"No one who is familiar with the life in these youth groups, can overlook the fact that here has begun between

---

[2] The part of the youth movement which is still religious in the fashion characteristic before the war is small if not miscroscopical.

the sexes relationship which would have been utterly impossible thirty years ago." [3]

In this change which has occurred in the last thirty years, particularly in the last ten, there is not only a new attitude toward sex which is to be stressed, but also an intense interest in the possibilities of an entire reconstruction in the mode of living. Sex, however fundamental, is but one mode, and in order to make its own reconstruction effective, other modes of behavior must experience the same reconstructive process. Youth is engaged in a struggle against an inelastic and ossified ethic. It has taken arms against authority and tradition.

In this study of Herr Hodann, which we previously cited, we learn that the youth movement has already condemned "the Christian concept of morals which was embedded in our bones," in its dedication to the new ethic in which "the innumerable anxieties of adolescence are beginning to disappear in the joyful recognition of Eros." German youth is not flirting in the quiet obscurity of the dark, but has declared its challenge in the unconcealing and candid daylight. It has not endeavored to effect companionate marriages in secret, and deny them in public. It has sought its salvation,

[3] "The Erotic Problem in the Bourgeois Youth Movement," Herr Hodann; translated from the German.

and redemption from the old stupidities, in recognition rather than deception.

"Redemption can be found only in the acknowledgment of life with all of its manifestations. That which makes life worthwhile is the passion with which we live it, it is the intensity of the experiences of which it consists. I know I shall be misunderstood. Perhaps some will interpret my desire as that of a degenerate—the cry for the liberty of a roué. Fools who know so little of the fire that is living in our youth! Anyone who has only the faintest inkling of the possibilities that are here, still unearthed, can only wish that the last vestiges which have been carried over from past ages, may disappear before Eros—that life should be lived as it is, because we want it just as it is." [4]

The youth-movement and the new sex mores serve as the principal motivation of multitudes of books, pamphlets, and treatises. It is one of the most consuming topics of the day. Indeed, one can scarcely glance through a Germany newspaper or magazine, or allow his eyes to run along the shelves of a book-store or library, without being confronted with some suggestion of this theme or allusion to its influence. Every angle of the movement has been subjected to dissection and diagnosis.

Ibid.

"There is hardly another problem which is as much subject to discussions and disquisitions, as the problem of sexual relations. Can it be otherwise? Are not the questions it raises, the questions of sexual mores, questions that touch the whole range of human problems? At all times, among all nations, they have moved and absorbed men, and the development and growth, or decline and destruction of a nation have depended more closely upon their solution than upon wars, famines, or epidemics. However often a solution may be found, it is of no help to succeeding generations. Each nation and age must take up these problems anew." [5]

These words are taken from a pamphlet that has reached wide audiences in Germany, and which, in consideration of its fundamentally religious character, attests the interests that the sex-problem has now awakened. Its author, Nelly Lutz, is a moralist if not a puritan. Yet she is cognizant of changes in the world in which she lives. She perceives the trend of youth, and is anxious to check and direct it. The exuberance of youth in things secular rather than in things sacred inspires her conscience to action. Let us observe her description of this new tendency among the youth of Germany since the war:

"And what is to be understood by their desires? . . . They want absolute freedom from restraint in their sexual

[5] "Unsolved Problems," Nelly Lutz; translated from the German.

[212]

relations. They want to live; they want to be free and 'love' whom and how they wish, and they live this life publicly, without evasion or shame. . . . Particularly in educated circles do they place great stress upon it. . . . They talk about ideal matters: about liberty and the holy right of youth; they rationalize their acts and defend them. They attack the idea of feminine innocence and purity, of faithfulness in marriage, and the duties of a wedded life—and all of this attack in the name of a higher morality. They utilize the simple method of calling moral that which they do, so that what hitherto may have been done secretly, accompanied by pangs of conscience, in fear of shame and disgrace, is now done openly, without handicap, in the broad daylight."

This description of the new youth and its attitude has unusual value in aiding us to interpret the direction of current customs in contemporary Germany. In the first place, we must not forget that the author is a woman who deplores all this which she is forced to see in the life that surrounds her, and which in a later sentence she attacks by saying that "even the most beautiful words cannot make an ugly thing beautiful." Were she a romantic radical we might suspect her of exaggeration in defense of Utopia. As it is, she recognizes these tendencies only with regret. The sentence that is especially instructive is the one in which she stresses the fact that those sex-relations which once were hidden because of the public obloquy that accompanied their exposure, are now admitted without hesitancy or tergiversation. Under the old mores sex-expression was concealed when it was not legal; under the new, as we have seen, it is in Germany without the hypocrisy and deceit of the clandestine and the camouflaged.

One of the conflicts that was conspicuous in the old morality was the discrepancy between economics and impulse. In our earlier chapter on Companionate Marriage we considered this discrepancy in detail, and its costs as part of a suppressive ethic. This old code of bourgeois morality, Elizabeth Busse-Wilson, writes:

"refused to compromise its forms of behavior, and demanded that people who are in love must restrain themselves until economic conditions permit a legitimate satisfaction of their sexual urge. Let youth be sacrificed, and let the roads and streets be crowded with the bodies of those martyred to this prescription—but the law must be upheld." Here is the iconoclastic response of youth, in reply to the old logic:

"They love each other intensely, unspeakably. They would like so much to belong to each other wholly—but it is impossible. Economic conditions do not permit their marriage, or social conditions are of such a character that marriage is out of the question. Should they wait with uncertain prospects and waste the most beautiful years of their youth? Should they part and ruin themselves in longing, and break up their bodies and souls? Or should those forces be right who say: 'If two people love, nothing must keep them from living for and with each other. The idea that people belong to each other only in marriage is antiquated. The sexual problem is beyond good and evil, the sexual urge is as natural as eating and drinking; we are sex-beings; we may follow our inherent nature.' How self-evident it sounds! Is it not really unjust if custom interferes with two people, who believe they are born for each other? Is it not unjust to repress the sexual life?" [6]

The answer of youth is one of affirmation. Freedom from suppression is the new motto. Emancipation from the old mores is the new aspiration. This cry for freedom and emancipation has already raced from audacity to defiance.

"With youth sex-freedom is justified . .·. and accepted as a fact. . . . It has become Körperseele, the unity of Logos and Eros." [7]

[6] *Ibid.* It is curious to note that this is described by one who is not in sympathy with the logic expressed.

[7] *"Woman and Youth Movement,"* Elizabeth Busse-Wilson. A commentary on feminine characteristics and a criticism of anti-feminism. Published by Free German Youth.

Challenge is written through the whole revolt. Marriage as an institution and form of moral behavior is scorned as antiquated and artificial.

"There are now no seducers and no seduced. The girl who gives love for love, who gives her love without desire for ulterior compensations, is no more taboo. It is, indeed, repulsive to the sentiment of the girl to mar emotional tension by the cold requests of codes and compensations." [8]

In those words we are brought face to face with the real nature of the new morals. Sex is no longer sacred except for the spontaneity of mutual attraction that is involved in its expression. The idea of codes and compensations, that is, of moral virtue and marriage, is impertinent and unexquisite. It introduces a calculating element into a relationship that should be free of all impediments that tend to rob or mar its beauty. In this aspiration, there is not, as is often maintained, an attempt to physicalize love, but an endeavor to

[8] *Ibid.* In passing it is of value to point out that in almost every instance in which we discover denunciations of this new freedom of German youth, they come from those connected with the Church and the sundry activities related to its craft. Wilhelm Stahlin, for instance, who is almost hysterical at times in his defense of the old and attack upon the new, is a clergyman of the old school, and author of such books as "Jesus and Youth," and "The Cross of Christ." Nelly Lutz is connected with a Bible Students' organization. Their conservatism, therefore, is not an unexpected reaction. In their very criticism, however, they attest the existence of the freedom which they decry.

spiritualize it. This endeavor differs as much from the license of the libertine as from the prudishness of the puritan.

"Modern youth does not consider physical love as a bodily satisfaction of a low order, as a purely animal function, but as a spiritual experience. It has found again a new awe before the sexual act, which sanctifies the love-experience in itself. The sexual is no more labeled 'wicked' and needs no theological justification to hallow it. Love has no other 'aim' besides itself. Yet sex cannot fulfill itself, free from spiritual existence; there arises rather a new unity out of this re-accomplished union of the sexual and the spiritual: 'Körperseele.'

"Fundamentally no 'new' ethics was required to cause the revolt of the young generation against the bourgeois sex life. Yet it was needed (this new ethics) only to free love from its chains." [9]

---

[9] This quotation is also taken from Elizabeth Busse-Wilson. ("The New Ethics") In her study "Woman and the Youth Movement" she has written a very illuminating survey of certain of the more salient tendencies in the youth movement. She analyzes trends and discusses their danger as well as advantage in the development of a German youth, free in fact as well as in form. She is anxious that certain tendencies toward the exaltation of homosexual affection among youths, an exaltation often justified upon intellectual grounds fortified with historical fact, akin in its argument often to the logic of Plato in the "Symposium,"—she is anxious that this homosexual affection be replaced by a heterosexual affection far more intense than the sweetest ecstasies in Lesbos.

In Frank Thiess's recent novel "The Gateway to Life," one finds the spirit of the German youth movement delineated in rich detail. It is a drama of the new ethics. The new attitudes toward sex, purity and virtue, are evident and conspicuous in almost every situation and emotional struggle. In these fragmentary sentences one can detect the same attitude that we found in the pamphlets which we discussed in earlier paragraphs:

"But isn't it debasing to lose your purity?"

"What do I care what people call debasing? Every act is as pure, or as simple, as the man that commits it. As the hour that follows it. Do you understand? The virtuous who can do nothing else and then make a morality of their impotence, I find the most hateful of all."

.   .   .   .   .   .

"Love? Yes. You may love everything. Who shall put your feelings in chains?"

This same sentiment, it should be added, is to be found elsewhere than in the youth movement. In Blucher's "Die Rolle der Erotic in der Männlichen Gessellschaft," we find statements of this character:

"A woman who commits adultery only exchanges her status of a prostitute, in which she finds herself in bourgeois mercenary marriage, for that of final dignity and freedom." [10]

This struggle for a new way of life which we find so marked in the aims and aspirations of German youth is but part of a deep-moving revolutionary upheaval that has begun to manifest itself in every activity of the modern world. Its economic background is obvious. The decadence of the bourgeoisie, and its morality, made revolt against its ethical code inevitable. German youth has carried this revolt beyond the confusion of its earlier forms. It has given a certain formulation to its freedom. It has striven to fuse a certain idealism into its protest, embody a certain philosophy in its revolt. In this way it has endeavored to preserve its emancipation from chaos, and its freedom from anarchy and self-indulgence.

[10] Even in legal circles the air is resonant with moral revolt. In his book "Divorce Laws of the Future," Dr. F. Trauman, attorney at law of the Supreme Court at Düsseldorf, has voiced something of the spirit of this new attitude. In discussing the advisability of granting divorce upon the basis of mutual consent, he asseverates:

"Ethics and common sense meet here, as so often happens, hand in hand. Therefore this is not a weird hypothetical suggestion, but only the logical deduction from the recognition of liberty as a fundamental principle of the present phase of love, which has reached a stage where it has become a matter of individual choice."

In another paragraph of his treatise he adds, with signal emphasis, that the "superannuated conceptions of the dying age are slowly being replaced by the path-finding spirit of the new epoch."

THE NEW MORALITY IN SOVIET RUSSIA

CHAPTER XII

Revolutionary Chaos and Change

WHAT we have seen in the preceding chapters of our study, has been a decay of an old morality; what we shall see in Soviet Russia, will be a rise of the new. In many countries, as we have observed, there have been numerous attempts to amend the old morals, and lend a flexibility to their form; and in general provide ways in which men and women can adjust themselves to the new changes in life without a total sacrifice of the old manners and morals. That these attempts have often proven ineffective is obvious. At the same time, however, it should be noted that many countries have begun to take a more enlightened attitude toward the entire moral problem. For instance, the Scandinavian countries have been in advance of the United States, as well as many other western countries. Nevertheless these changes in Sweden, Denmark, and Norway have not marked a very revolutionary progression. In North Dakota, the advance in reference to the problem of illegitimacy has been equally progressive. North Dakota, of course, provides an extreme exception. On the whole, then, whatever has been attempted in these western countries, has been in an endeavor to retain something of the old, even in its sacrifice of the new.

In Soviet Russia the situation is unique. While in other countries we note the general decay of the marriage order and the old morals, in the Soviet Union we discover a new attitude toward marriage, and the necessary freedoms that should underlie it, which eliminates utterly the element of decay. We, therefore, find a condition that is a remarkable and refreshing contrast. Although many of the ideals which are inherent in the system of life that is being worked out in this new society, are still far from attainment, at the same time the advance that has been made has been of a singularly revolutionary character. In commenting upon the exceptional changes that are to be discovered in Soviet morality, it is necessary to understand that the history of Russia since 1917, has been of a sufficiently chaotic character to impede continuous progress. For instance, Russia was more shaken by the war than any other nation. The war in Russia was followed by a series of crises, including counter-revolution, military intervention, and the famine, which all played a part in handicapping the advance of the people. For example, as a result of the war alone, Russia lost over 1,500,000 men, with another million and one-half incapacitated, as a consequence of wounds and disease; during the period of the Revolution, with the invasion of Denikin, Kolchak, and Wrangel, over 6,500,000 fatalities are recorded, and finally with the famine of 1921-22, 5,000,000 more lives were wiped out. Such losses were catastrophic. It has only been in the last three or four years that Soviet Russia has been able to make a recovery from this suffering and chaos.

In approaching the problem of morality in Soviet Russia, therefore, it must be understood that the ideals set forth in this new life have only had a brief period in which to crystallize. It is the astounding intelligence embodied in these ideals that it is our purpose to observe and study.[1]

In so many ways, Soviet Russia has served as a social and economic experiment for the world. In morality

---

[1] In referring to the intelligence embodied in these new laws, we are not for a moment considering intelligence as an abstract entity free of social and economic derivation. On the contrary, we are anxious to stress the fact that this intelligence has been achieved through the abandonment of the moral concepts and inhibitions of one social class, for the new concepts and criteria of another. If we do not always insist upon the phraseology of class-reference and attitude, it is not because we question the influence of class-conflict as the basic motivation in the entire moral process.

likewise, it has attempted more than an emendation of the old morals. The abuse which has been showered upon its new ideas has been unspeakably venomous. Its motivation has often been of a vicious character. The Sisson forgeries which attempted to foist upon the world the "nationalization of women" myth, is but one example of this abuse. So widespread has been the propaganda against the Soviet union, that the multitude in America still believe in this myth or something very similar to it. Although the United States Department of State on February 28, 1919 declared that the rumor as to the "nationalization of women" is not true, writers still return to this theme with a morbid avidity and enthusiasm. In a book entitled "The Red War on the Family," Mr. Samuel Saloman endeavors to confirm this myth. That his evidence is nugatory, his logic ridiculous, and his entire discussion shot through with silliness and ignorance, have little to do with the appeal and influence which such a book has exercised with the untutored. As late as June 12, 1927, the *New York American,* through the pen of Karl Wiegand, manufactured another canard of somewhat kindred variety. These canards are numerous. Their effect has been very unfortunate and profound. It shall be our aim to combat such misleading and fallacious evidence, not by attack, but by mere consideration of conditions and facts as they exist in Soviet Russia today.

Each age seems to suffer from the delusion of permanence. It mistakenly comes to accept its own order as final. Whatever opposes its own concepts meets with its denunciation. The attitude of the West towards the changes that have been effected in the marital code and marital life of Soviet Russia, is antagonistic, because these changes mark a decisive departure in the direction of a new morality. They are interlinked with the changes of an entire social order.

In problems such as marriage, divorce, illegitimacy, birth control, abortions, and prostitution, the attitude in Soviet Russia is very different from that in America and Europe. It is these differences which it is important to consider. It is in these differences that we shall find the early beginnings of a new moral outlook.

THE BACKGROUND OF THE OLD RUSSIAN MORALITY

It is necessary to understand the moral life in Russia prior to the Revolution in order to appreciate the significance of the new mores. The comparative ease with which the change from one morality to another was effected, can be understood only in terms of historical perspective. While the old morality had its hideous aspects in abundance, it is important to note that it also had its looseness and laxness as part of its structure. In early times according to Chronicle of Nestor, in the eleventh century, sexual life was very free and promiscuous. Side by side with promiscuity there grew up a practice of wife-stealing and wife-seizure, and the habit of having two or three wives was by no means uncommon. Festivals held at sacred times during the year, also held in many countries of western Europe, were conspicuous for their sexual abandon. Incest was not infrequent. Russian girls and Russian women possessed an extraordinary amount of sexual freedom. This freedom did not cease even with the coming of Christianity.[2]

Marriage for instance was a very easily arranged and very easily dissolved affair in the early days of Russian moral life. Later on, of course, this was considerably abridged, and, with the growing influence of Christianity, woman came to be looked upon as something of a sorceress, and her privileges were shortly seized. The Christian concept of sex as a sin and woman as the chief incarnation of it, rapidly grew into a belief. Woman, therefore, soon became nothing more than a slave. Just as Plato had classified women with cattle,

[2] For much of the information in reference to early family life in Russia, I am deeply indebted to a very excellent study of this subject, made by Elaine Elnett, "Historic Origin and Social Development of Family Life in Russia."

the Russian developed the same attitude. Wife-beating became the natural custom. "The husband ought to teach his wife with love and sensible punishment"; such was the advice of the Domostroy, the moral Baedecker of the sixteenth century. The wife was subservient to the husband in every form of behavior. The sale of wives was a frequent procedure. Women were isolated from the company of men, except with their husbands in their homes. The proverbs themselves give interesting evidence of the attitude that existed toward women. "Not to beat a woman is not to get any good out of her"; "Hit your wife and the soup will be tastier"; "Beat your wife while she is young and you shall have rest in your old age"—such are a few of the proverbs that grew up in reference to wives and women.

Other proverbs illustrate the same contempt for women: "A chicken is not a bird: a woman is not a human being"; "Girls are not human beings: goats are not cattle." Woman's intelligence was viewed in no kindlier fashion. "A woman's hair is long, and her brain is short," is typical of the masculine opinion of the era. Woman was not to be trusted. A score of proverbs justify this attitude.

This attitude toward woman is part of a man-made morality in which marriage was a form of purchase,

[229]

and in which match-makers were an established institution.

While these conditions existed among the peasants, there is a different story to be told about the women of the upper classes. Here a freedom and a liberty existed that were indeed singular in the so-called Christian world. Women were active in the professional classes, medical and pedagogical, long before women in other countries were able to attain the privilege of education. They thus set an example that was not without its meaning in the history of the modern woman. Their attitude toward morality was exceptionally latitudinarian. Women also played a vital part in the revolutionary movement. They were active in Cossack revolts, the insurrection of the Novgorod military settlers, and in the terroristic plots against noble and Tzar. Thousands of them were exiled in Siberia or incarcerated in prison and fortress. Such figures as Vera Figner and Sophia Perovskaya were examples of the flaming efforts of Russian women to destroy an ancient tyranny and oppression.

In morality, the revolt of Russian women was not less resolute. Their social heritage made insurrection less difficult. The economic background did not accentuate the puritanic virtues. Virginity was never a precious and indispensable attribute. The western concept of chastity seemed silly and superfluous in a country removed from the carking astringencies of a bourgeois morality. Among the peasants, promiscuity of sexual relations in early times had never entirely ceased. Even in this century, the old custom of *jus primus noctis* is still often continued. It is far more prevalent in Great Russia than in Little Russia. The thrifty, economic virtues of the English bourgeoisie, for example, in a civilization which was without the race and rush of great commerce and industry, had little attraction. The bourgeois groups in Russia were a decided minority. The George Sandist movement in Russia had a far-reaching and pervasive influence. The upper-class women rose in revolt against the withering conditions of their era. Seduction, adultery, and the liaison became romantically popular. The women rulers that followed Peter the Great exercised no little part in the changes that occurred. The wife who once could have been forced by her husband into a convent now turned to a bawdy poet for romantic escape. The Domostroy became amusingly archaic. The bobbed-hair revolt took place in Russia many generations ago. Bobbed hair and an independent mien became associated with the idea of emancipation. Fictitious marriages for the sake of fuller freedom of action were a frequent resort. The Russian women of the upper classes, then, had early developed a spirit of protest and resistance, which had long died in the soul of the peasant woman.

As early as the first part of the eighteenth century, Peter the Great had founded a hospital for illegitimate children. Only in the last few generations has the west adopted such measures of protection for children born out of wedlock. Catherine the Great had looked with a certain sweetness upon the illegitimate child and treated him in somewhat gentler terms than her predecessors. It was this same Catherine who in this dark and barbarous country first endeavored to carry out the old theory of taking away children from their parents and educating them in government schools and colleges. Her ideal, it should be remembered, was not modelled upon the Spartan concept. She was eager to have children escape the oppression of the family, the parental stupidities and affections. Such revolutionary departures from ordinary ethical customs made a firm and fixed moral code in Russia impossible.

These extraordinary conditions with both peasantry and aristocracy, made change, reform, and revolution in morals an easy somersault. Where rigidities were absent, changing customs and concepts can be more easily and rapidly accepted. In this way it is not difficult to understand how readily and completely the Russians have been able to adopt the new morals of the revolution.

Those who maintain today that Soviet Russia is going to change its policy and return to the puritanism of the past, argue without historical knowledge or intelligence. Their contention is ridiculous. They speak in terms of a western concept with which Russia has never been fastly fettered. That the peasant is to be turned into a puritan is an amusing absurdity, touching to those who know his past and present. The unintelligent freedom of an old morality, however, will be converted into the intelligent freedom of a new.

A MORALITY FOR WOMEN

Morality in the past has been made by man for the subordination of woman. If this statement seems something of an exaggeration, historical fact and ethical theory do not repudiate it. With the exception of certain periods in the history of primitive man, a few intervals in the career of the ancient world, a brief episode at the close of the Roman empire, the history of morality has been the history of male supremacy. Women have been ruthlessly ground beneath this Juggernaut of masculine morality. If men did not always consciously endeavor to subordinate woman, the effects of their mores were none the less conducive to that end. In many cases the intention is obvious by the very deceptions employed to frighten and terrify the women. A multitude of devices were actually designed for the perpetuation of feminine submission. These ceremonies were ingenious. At the time of initiation, for instance, the boys were introduced to the mystery of Tundun's roar. Tundun's roar [3] is then seen to be nothing other than an artifice of deception. It is not the roar of Tundun, but the noise of bullroarers made by men. The women are never initiated into this mystery. They continue to be cowed by it until death. In such ways are women subordinated in primitive society by men. In later society, as with the Greeks, for instance, custom had already subjected her to an enslaved position. The relative advantages which she had under Hammurabi, for example, or even under the Egyptians, are eclipsed by the civilized man of later centuries. Christianity only tightened her fetters. The priesthood associated her with the devil, and her ways with those of wickedness. While among the Jews *she had been placed in the same category with a man's ox, ass, and other private property*, with the Christian ecclesiastic she became a temptress and curse.

[3] "A Short History of Women," Langdon-Davies.

Even in more modern societies, her position was not greatly improved. As culture advanced, the subjection of woman was not relaxed. Even such a revolutionary as Rousseau conceived of woman as a being made for no other purpose than to be pleasing and agreeable to man. The English frowned upon women who sought education as an ideal. Ignorance and innocence went better with the sweet submissiveness desired in women than knowledge and sophistication. Women were nothing other than forms of chattel, even in highly moral England. She was the virtual slave of her husband.[4]

Let us examine the condition of women in England a little more closely before proceeding to the situation in Soviet Russia. English morality is often foolishly exalted as an ideal. Its loftiness has been frequently commended to less civilized nations. Moralists never cease alluding to it as a criterion. This logic is sheer folly. Few countries have treated women worse, or degraded them as completely as modern England. Women in the days of Hammurabi had more freedom and privilege than in the days of George Eliot. Let us begin with the time of Ethelred for an introduction into the nature of the English ethic.

[4] Cf. author's "Sex Expression in Literature," pp. 222, 223; J. S. Mill's "The Subjection of Women."

Ethelred's attitude toward women is unmistakable. To him she was a piece of property to be bought or sold at the caprice of the owner. If a man seduced the wife of another, Ethelred required that the guilty pay the husband a fine and provide him another wife. The exact wording of the law is interesting and curious: "If a freeman have been familiar with a freeman's wife, let him pay for it with his wergild and provide another wife with his own money and bring her home to the other." In other words, the seduction of a wife was far more serious as a violation of property than of person. The sexual violation in itself was a matter of light consequence. It could be easily paid for and the provision of another wife was only a further fortification of the propertied aspect of the entire matter. At this time extra-marital relations between men and women were exceptionally popular.[5] Wife-sale and wife-purchase were part of the general business of the community. The number of such sales multiplied no doubt high into the hundreds of thousands, if not millions. This traffic was in no sense incompatible with the attitude toward women and the nature of morality that existed at the time. Women were valued at specific prices according to their respective qualifications. One of the factors that determined

[5] Wright, "Domestic Manners."

her value was her economic position in society. A widow, for example, was worth half as much as a virgin. In order to distinguish degrees of value in widowhood, four classes were denoted: those in the first class cost fifty shillings; in the second, twenty; in the third, twelve; in the fourth, six. The poorer classes, therefore, very often had to accept a widow instead of a virgin. Fathers were often ranked according to the number of daughters that they possessed, because their daughters represented potential capital.[6] Every woman at this time had to be under the guardianship of some man who was called her "mundbora" or guard. The father was, of course, the *guard* of his unmarried daughters. At his death his brother replaced him; then in the event of the brother's death came the next relative, and in one way or another, women were subject to some man, or men. The subordination of women was unquestionable.

The purchase-marriage had become universal in England at the time that Christianity was introduced and it did not by any means cease with the coming of this new religion. Ethelred's law was an evidence of its continuance. *As late as 1884,* twenty cases of wife-purchase, with the names, details of prices, some of

---

[6] F. S. Merryweather, "Glimmerings in the Dark, or Lights and Shadows of the Olden Times." London, 1850.

them varying between twenty-five guineas and a half pint of beer, are recorded. Accounts of such marriages are extraordinarily frequent, and a number of them startle by their very candour. Jeaffreson tells of avaricious fathers who often sold their handsome daughter to three or four suitors, and after having received payments for her, later sold her to another purchaser for a still higher sum. Sometimes daughters were sold while still children, and thus subterfuge was even easier. Women were often offered for sale in the newspapers. In a Dublin paper, for instance, women were frequently offered for sale under the inviting caption:

A BARGAIN TO BE SOLD

Women were usually led by their husbands with a rope about the neck, to the market place where they were sold along with cattle with the proper witnesses to sanction the bargain. A court clerk would determine the tax which seldom amounted to more than several shillings. Women thus lead about the market place by a rope became a common sight. Smithfield Market became famous for such sales. In connection with such sales, a very edifying note appeared in the *Times* on July 22nd, 1797:

"The increasing value of the fair sex is regarded by many writers as the certain index of a growing civilization. Smithfield may for this reason claim to be a contributor to particular progress in finesse, for in the market the price was again raised from one half a guinea to three-and-one-half."

This comment pictures the position of woman without equivocation. She was certainly nothing other than a bargain for bidders, an economic asset that fluctuated with changing conditions. In several English newspapers, interesting expressions of this attitude are to be discovered. In one London paper, for instance, a man advertised on one day the loss of a horse, offering a reward of five guineas for its return; on the next day, by a strange freak of the fortuitous, his wife ran away, and he inserted in the same paper an advertisement offering a reward of four shillings for her recovery.[7] The church was not at all immune from such traffic. In February, 1790, for instance, a wife, who had been deserted by her husband and had become a burden upon the parish, which had been supporting her, was sold at the market-place by the parishioners for two shillings. In the account of the transaction, even the cost of the rope was included. Such cases were familiar throughout England. In Nottingham during the year 1790, the cheapest woman sold was for three pence.

[7] "Das Geschlechtsleben in England," E. Duhren.

[239]

One case is of particular interest. A peasant who sold his wife at one time without formality, was informed that the sale was not legal; he thereupon went seven miles for his former wife, tied her with a rope, and again sold her, this time with due legal formality for one-half a crown. He was taxed by the state four pence duty—as he would have been for the sale of cattle.

The prevalence of fleet-marriages and the romantic marriages of Gretna Green also shed light upon the attitude toward marriage that was then extant. Three thousand of such fleet-marriages—deriving their name from the Fleet jail in the district of Fleet Ditch in which these marriages were performed—occurred in four months during the year of 1704.[8] These fleet-marriages were perpetrated often in a most low and vile fashion. The Gretna Green marriages increased and were not finally stopped by law until 1856. Matrimonial ads were also a popular device in England. Many of the agencies that were active in such advertising were based upon pure swindle. In one way or another woman was exploited, as is always the case with moralities that are made for men.

We see that the entire past of women has been fettered. The exceptions have been rare. Civilized

[8] "England and Scotland," by Fanny Lewald. Berlin, 1864.

[240]

morality did not improve her condition until she rose herself, armed by economic resource, in protest against her suppression. Today, however, in spite of the vote which she has acquired in a number of countries, her position is still inferior to that of man. Divorce laws have not lost their inequalities in sex privilege. Although the development of the new woman, and the rise of the new morality, have rapidly destroyed the double code of morals, at the same time, it is still the woman who primarily suffers for misfortune or mistake. In the economic world discrimination in favor of men still continues in open fashion.[9]

In Soviet Russia, for the first time in the history of the modern world, this inequality has been ended. Indeed, we may say that while morality in the past has been made for men, *morality in Soviet Russia is made for women.* In no other place in the so-called civilized world is the welfare of women given primary consideration. It may be accurately said that in all relations that come within the category of morality, legal statute has been invariably designed for the protection of women rather than men. This in itself constitutes a revolution in moral life and ethical theory and practice.

[9] The subjection of women, of course, was an expression of the economic structure of the society. In a world of class-struggle in which private-property dominated, the enslavement of women was inevitable.

The attitude of western nations, in its criticisms of morality in Soviet Russia presents us with a farcical contradiction. These moral minds of the West who have branded Soviet Russia as the country in which women are nationalized, and the wife has become the prostitute, are among the clowns of the era. From England, for instance, comes a host of moral philippics. The fulminations of these Anglo-Saxon virtuosi of virtue are brimful of hatred and ignorance. While in England, as we have seen, women have been treated as bond servants, bartered and sold like cattle, disesteemed and scorned, in Soviet Russia they have been really emancipated. It is indeed amusing if not strange, to observe men who have the history of their own country as a denial of the very ideals that they extol, assail Soviet Russia for things that have never occurred, and which, even if they had occurred, would not have been any worse than the conditions which have been prevalent in their own land.

Soviet Russia has not nationalized women; it has not bought and sold women; it has not bound them by law; it has not enslaved them by custom; it has not trafficked in their domestic relations and profited upon taxes thereby derived—in other words, it has freed and not fettered women.

Now let us see in just what ways this freedom has

been achieved. In the first place, woman is protected against the predatory tendencies of men. The laws that have been passed in reference to women have been laws which have aimed to endow women with legal prerogatives greater often than those of men.

Lenin's own words on this point are signal:

"It is a fact that in the course of the past ten years not a single democratic party in the world, not one among the leaders of the bourgeois republic, has undertaken for the emancipation of women the hundredth part of what has been realized by Russia in one year. All the humiliating laws prejudicial to the rights of women have been abolished: for example, those which made divorce difficult, the repugnant rules for inquiring into paternity, and other regulations, relating to illegitimate children. Such laws are in force in all civilized states to the shame of the bourgeoisie and capitalism. We are justly proud of our progress in this field. But as soon as we had destroyed the foundations of bourgeois laws and institutions we arrived at a clear conception of the preparatory nature of our work destined solely to prepare the ground for the edifice which was to be built; we have not yet come to the construction of the building."

In pre-revolutionary Russia the proverb, which we cited before: "A chicken is not a bird; a woman is not a human being," expressed the contempt in which woman

[243]

was held. This contempt was similar to that which existed in England where the custom of wife-purchase was its dominant manifestation. In Soviet Russia the change has been tremendous. The condition of women has been revolutionized. Such proverbs and such practices have become absurd and impossible. Woman at last has become a human being with the same rights and privileges as man.

Women is the equal of man in every activity and every organization of life. When she marries she is still a free woman; marriage, the domestic code clearly asserts, "does not establish community of property between the married persons"; and in another section we discover that "change of residence by one of the parties to a marriage shall not impose an obligation upon the other party to follow the form." The surname of the children may be that of either the wife or the husband, depending upon the voluntary decision of the couple. Hitherto in modern times, the surname of the child was necessarily that of the father. The right of the mother to take part in the decision of a name was totally inconceivable. As to change of residence, the right of the woman to refuse to follow her husband was equivalent to insubordination in the eyes of the modern world. Today in Soviet Russia, such refusal expresses nothing more than the natural right

for independence on the part of the woman as well as
the man. In political life woman's position is the
same as that of the man. The same is true in economic
life, within or without the trade unions. In education
the same condition prevails. There is no form of life
in which there is to be found an exception.

In the relations between the sexes the woman is again
afforded the main protection. In the matter of divorce
the woman's rights are in every detail equal to the
man's. With children the woman is completely protected. This protection, it should be emphasized, is
not limited to certain narrow phases of life, but in-
cludes within its scope every possibility of reaction.
The mother is protected whether her child is the result of a registered marriage or an unregistered. There
is no distinction or discrimination between so-called
legitimate and illegitimate. There are no illegitimate
children in Soviet Russia. As S. M. Glikin wrote:

"We have no legal and illegal children. Here all children
are equal, they are all legal." [10]

Whether a civil marriage has been performed or not,
man and woman are registered as father and mother in
the Bureau of Births. A family according to Soviet
law is "where there are parents and at least one

[10] "The New Law Concerning Family, Divorce, Marriage, and
Guardianship" (Soviet Pamphlet).

[245]

child." [11]   The woman thus cannot suffer the stigma which the western world thrusts upon the illegitimate mother.   All women and all mothers are equal before the law and in society.   This is an economic and moral consideration of vast significance.   It means that the woman no longer has to suffer a penalty that the man could formerly escape.   Their child is protected by the father, or in the event that the father cannot be located, which is very rare, by the State.   The moral onus which the western woman has had to bear in this respect has been costly and terrific.   This onus is removed in Soviet Russia.

The protection given the mother in the case of pregnancy is once more entirely inclusive.   Moral discriminations between married and unmarried mothers are, of course, non-existent.   Both before and after birth she is given time away from work, ranging from six to eight weeks, with pay and with medical attention.   In addition to her full pay she receives an extra stipend for food.   After the mother returns to work she is permitted a half hour in every three and a half hours to feed and care for her child.   This advantage alone signifies an advance toward a more progressive ethic.

In a later chapter we shall discuss more extensively the benefits which women have derived in Soviet Russia

[11] *Ibid.*

from the new ideas and laws which have been organized in reference to the problems of divorce, birth control, abortions, and prostitution. With each problem it is the woman that is favored. The woman's welfare is the determining criterion.

This new freedom which woman has acquired in Soviet Russia is a freedom that has manifested itself in practice as well as theory. Fifty thousand women now hold public office in Soviet Russia. Two hundred women are presidents of village Soviets. Five hundred thousand women are factory delegates. There are women factory managers who each have as many as one thousand workers under them. In the higher professional colleges, studying such subjects as engineering, medicine, economics and art, women constitute thirty-five percent of the student body. Women judges are numerous. The Russians, in fact, encourage women to occupy posts in courts, to help rule and adjudicate matters in the country and share evenly in all other activities with men. Madame Kollontai, formerly ambassador to Mexico, now to Norway,[12] is the first woman plenipotentiary ever sent out by a modern country as representative to a foreign power.

---

[12] She had been sent to Norway for the first time before being despatched to Mexico. This is her second residence as Soviet plenipotentiary in Norway.

An enormous change thus has occurred in the life of woman in Russia. She has seen more than the dawn of a new age. In no other country has she attained such freedom and privilege. While at one time the husband beat the wife, and this was considered the custom, now the wife reports her husband's conduct to the president of the Soviet if he doesn't behave, and a paper comes to the husband summoning him for correction. Morality is then no longer a morality made by men, it is as much a morality made for women.

CHAPTER XIII

LOVE, MARRIAGE AND DIVORCE

I T is not in the problems of love, marriage, and divorce that the advance in morality in Soviet Russia has been most direct and decisive. Love and the sex life have been freed of the superstitions and silences which had clouded, confused, and bound them; marriage has been liberated from the religious and ceremonial rites in which it had once been bound; divorce has been converted into an intelligent device, disenslaved from duplicity and deceit and accessible to all. As a result, morality has been emancipated from the stereotyped stupidities of an enforced convention and an inelastic code.

Love and the sex life are looked upon in Soviet Russia as the private privilege of the individual, and not the concern of the state. This attitude, which English moralists, such as Havelock Ellis, Bertrand Russell and Edward Carpenter, in the vanguard of their contemporaries, have urged in theory, the Russians have put into practice. This achievement is phenomenal. It marks the introduction of an intelligence into morals that is noteworthy and significant. The sex-life of individuals is not to be subject to supervision or punishment. It is only when children are involved that the relation becomes a social matter, and necessitates the intervention of the state. This intervention, it should be added, is always in behalf of the woman, and every law concerning it is designed for her protection. The history of moral standards, in the west, particularly during the last three hundred years, has been one of close restrictions and confinements. Love and the sex-life, once bartered for a dowry or sold for a shilling, had been regulated by law and rigid social custom. The individual had to fit his impulse into this organized and unnatural order of behavior. In Soviet Russia suffering occasioned by the conflict between economics and impulse has been dissolved.

The education of the individual in sex begins at an early age. Sex instruction is part of the general curriculum in every educational institution of consequence. This instruction is characterized by a candor that endeavors to destroy the foolish confusions and absurdities which ordinarily grow up about the topic in the minds of western youth. This instruction is not instruction obfuscated by analogy and impaired by properly punctuated omissions. When we recall the statements which we quoted in an earlier chapter in reference to the wisdom of such instruction for youths in America, an excellent idea of contrast between prudishness and candor, between convention and reason, between superstition and science, is provided. The American scientist who disapproved of a thorough study in the anatomical differences between the sexes is a splendid example of the surrender of intelligence to custom. Such an attitude is not only absurd, but it is nothing more than a foolish memory of an unenlightened past—in Soviet Russia. It is for this reason that children grow up in that country with an understanding of sex that is uncharacterized by pruriency and evasion. Such instruction after all must be the basis for any sensible study of the problem of sex. Such instruction must begin in youth if it is to be effective in combatting the myth and mystery in which sex has been hitherto enveiled. Without it love and the sex life can never be felicitous and exquisite.

Despite our conventions, customs, and codes, men have been mastered by sex, and not the masters of it. The disruption of the old code in the western world represents only an increasingly concentrated revolt against a set of moral regulations. Preceding this contemporary revolt were the untold individual revolts which were scorned by society, castigated by law, but which had nevertheless not ceased. The double standard of morality evinced likewise the incompatibility of moral regulations with masculine impulse—the male revolted, however, because he could afford to revolt; the female did not revolt because she could not afford it. Now that she can afford it, too, she has revolted also. Sex reaction under the double code became distorted and its expression ruined by monotony or often aberration. The costs of suppression, and the deceptions occasioned by its violation, have left their imprints, deep and often ineradicable in the nervous structure of modern man. Our neurotic and psychotic age, as we have previously pointed out, is closely connected with this suppression. No sane sex ethic could arise from such a moral outlook. It was only by destroying the concealments that had been perpetuated about sex in the minds of youth, removing the suppressions that had been urged and enforced by bourgeois society, that Soviet Russia has been able to erect a new ethical edifice. Ignorance had to be supplanted by knowledge, suppression had to be removed, and spontaneity of impulse had to replace conformities of conduct.

The new laws regarding marriage and divorce in Soviet Russia have been constructed in such a manner as to provide for the expression of this new attitude.

Marriage and divorce are freer in Soviet Russia than in any other part of the western world. Notwithstanding this advance, even these laws do not yet attain this ideal. As M. I. Kalinin said:

"The new law is not entirely new. It only makes a big step forward."[1] Or as stated in the early edition of the code:

"Only time and experience will show how many of the provisions of this code belong to the transitional category, features which are destined to banish with the more perfect establishment of the socialist order. In certain clauses, however, there is clearly to be discerned a conscious recognition of conditions and habits of life surviving from the old order. Such survivals are inevitable at this time when neither the economic nor psychological transformation is complete. There are provisions respecting property and income which will inevitably be subject to obsolescence or amendment. The law of guardianship, essentially revolutionary as it is, is yet no more than a first tentative approach to the realization of collective responsibility for the care of the young. The laws of marriage and divorce still bear traces of the passing order, frank and sensible acknowledgment of the existence of certain economic and psychological conditions only to be overcome when the complete change is accomplished."

[1] Quoted from "Marriage and Family," A. Prigradov-Kudrin. (Soviet Publication)

[253]

If all the traces of the old order have not been eradicated from the new marriage laws in the Soviet Union, the mythical, magical and religious aspects have certainly been discarded. Marriage now is only a civil procedure. While couples may still be married by a religious ceremony, their action is not legal until it has undergone civil sanction. The religious rite, which is discouraged, is unessential; the civil alone is vital. Under the Tzar the opposite situation was conspicuous. If a man and woman lived together for thirty years, and had ten children, the couple could not appear as man and wife unless a church marriage was effected, nor could the children appear as progeny of the father. According to the old Russian law this man was not their father, and in the bureau of births these children were entered as born illegitimately, of an unknown father. The woman had no rights to the property of the man nor did his children; if he died intestate his property went to his relatives. In fact, according to penal statute, every woman who lived with a man, in an unmarried state, could be categorized as a "prostitute." [2] This condition of woman in Tzaristic Russia was akin to that in the England of the pure-passioned Victorians. Today in Soviet Russia such a condition harks back to the archaic. A

[2] *Ibid.*

man and woman, as we noted in the preceding chapters, are recorded as father and mother, whether their marriage is registered or not. The woman, therefore, suffers no isolation or scorn. Her child has the same rights and is looked upon in the same way whether she is married or unmarried. If she lives with a man without marriage, she is viewed in the same way as if she lives with a man to whom she is married. The registration of a marriage, therefore, has a statistical rather than a moral value.

This attitude toward marriage, which refuses to insert any distinction between registered or unregistered marriage, is indicative of how free marital relations are in Soviet Russia. The equalization of registered and unregistered marriage, for a time was a matter of anxious dispute. Many were opposed to equalizing the two types of marriage. At first only registered marriages were looked upon with favor and those who were registered as married had advantages over those who were unregistered. Soltz and Riazanov were sturdily opposed to this equalization of marriages. The controversy was exciting and hard-fought. Moirova, one of the women delegates active in this dispute, classified the contentions of Soltz and Riazanov as tainted with remains of bourgeois morality. Her words are a challenge-call:

[255]

"What are we? Bourgeois moralists, that we occupy ourselves with such a distinction?"

City groups were much more in favor of equalization than rural groups although at many of the village-meetings the vote was for abolition of all distinction. The question thus was debated in every part of Russia and it was the masses who finally decided in favor of the equalization of both types of marriage.[3]

Apropos of this dispute over registered and unregistered marriages, one of the statements made in the Ukraine, in protest against the advantage given to registered marriage, is astonishingly clear and concise in voicing the attitude in contemporary Russia:

"Marriage is a private act of the citizen which does not concern the state . . . a voluntary relationship made by two citizens."[4]

It should be mentioned also that before the masses voted in favor of equalization of registered and unregistered marriages, many statistics were adduced to stress the wisdom of such equalization. D. I. Kurski showed that in 1923 unregistered marriages far exceeded those registered; the actual ratio was 70,-000 to 100,000 unregistered. Furthermore, in a study

[3] *Ibid.*
[4] *Novy Mir.* February, 1927.

of 300 alimony cases in Moscow state court it was
found that 14 of the children resulted from casual relations, 41 from long cohabitation and 68 from short-
time cohabitation extending up to one year. It was
further estimated by Kurski that at least 15% of
couples living together did not register their marriage.

According to the new law, now, both registered
and unregistered marriages have the same right and
privilege.[5] The husband in an unregistered marriage
has the same rights and duties as in a registered; the
same is true of the wife. Before this equalization these
rights and duties did not exist. Then the right of
one person to be supported by the other in case of illness or inability to work did not obtain. Nor was
there the right of inheritance at death. The dissolution of these distinctions was a move of not a little
importance.

As in the discussion in reference to registered and
unregistered marriages, the consideration of the entire
marital code which now prevails in Soviet Russia was
discussed by the entire population before a decision
was consummated. The new marital code is not a de-

[5] An unregistered marriage is a marriage in which the relations re-
spond to the conditions in the code: Proofs of a marital cohabitation
before third parties in the form of personal correspondence and other
documents; the jointship of their property in this cohabitation, joint
upbringing of children, etc.

[257]

vice of one group or of one sex to foist a morality upon another. The workers and peasants discussed this marital code for a whole year before it was accepted. S. M. Glikin, describing the procedure, states:

"The All-Russian Central Ispolkom decided not to sanction the new law until it could be discussed by the workers. During a whole year the new laws were discussed in factories, shops, village-meetings, and military organizations. . . . The laboring masses of the Republic discussed it with great attention. . . . In its final form, thus, it represents the conclusions of millions of workers in cities and villages." [6]

The statement of another Soviet writer, Kudrin, is also pertinent:

"The new code of marriage and family is not only a law forged out by the hands of many millions of laboring people, but it also reflects the spirit of the revolutionary state."

Here is a morality, then, that actually expresses the voluntary desire and choice of a people. Over 6,000 debates on the subject were held in villages alone, and thousands more in towns and cities. It manifests the spirit of an epoch.

Marriage in the Soviet Union cannot bind the woman as it does in other countries. Woman's freedom is

[6] "The New Law Concerning Marriage, Family and Guardianship."

not a passive thing, but an active, dynamic reality. In the protest of Moirova flashes the assertiveness and independence of the new Russian woman: "After I read the statement in the code to the effect that the change of location of one of the spouses does not necessitate that the other follow him, I confess I could not understand why, ten years after the Revolution, this must be stated in a special article. Is it not understood that we live at such a time where we can choose as we please the place we desire? Are there still among us people who think that a wife must follow her husband? This is too much, comrades." Very often women sever themselves entirely from their old existence, demand a divorce, and forge their way into a freer life.[7] This revolt attests the growth of feminine resolution and intelligence. The working woman is constantly instructed in the nature of her rights, and in the importance of their expression. Her advance is cultivated as much as that of man. Marriage as a consequence can never become an institution of inequality, as it has been in the past, and still is in other nations.

With the removal of the religious element in marriage, and the establishment of the right of the woman

[7] I. A. Rostovsky, "New Law Concerning Marriage, Family and Guardianship." (Third Edition, Soviet Pamphlet.)

to obtain and determine the destiny of her property after marriage, the developments in divorce follow in natural sequence. Just as it is expected that in the "future Communist society of course there will be no registration of marriage at all," and that "if the code of 1918 made registration necessary, it did so only to fit the conditions of the moment, and as a transitory expedient," [8] in the laws pertaining to divorce, it has been necessary to insert, in particular reference to children, clauses that are still without the extraordinary freedom of the socialist ideal. Nevertheless, the most revolutionary factor of the new Russian mores is that of the free divorce. It is the advance made in this field which facilitates an easy future development for this entire ethic. Divorce can be got by mutual consent, or even at the instigation of one party, on the ground of incompatibility. The statement of the code is unambiguous:

"The mutual consent of the husband and wife or the desire of either of them to obtain a divorce shall be considered a ground for divorce."

Under the Tzar, divorce had been accessible only to the opulent. Today it is a liberating device, attainable by every worker and peasant in the Soviet Republics.

[8] Prigradov-Kudrin, "Marriage and Family." (Soviet Pamphlet.)

The collusion and camouflage that are necessitated in other countries, when the genuine reason for divorce is incompatibility, are superfluous in the Soviet Union. While in Switzerland divorce upon the basis of mutual consent is valid, there is not in the Swiss attitude the far-spanning vision that is embodied in the Russian. Absolute freedom in divorce is the Russian ideal. Divorce should always be, unless there are children involved, the concern of the individuals themselves and no one else. Artifice and subterfuge are at once hostile and alien to this concept. They stultify its theory. The freedom of divorce in Soviet Russia, therefore, has been expanded to a maximum. As S. M. Glikin avers:

"Soviet divorce is so free that if one of the parties wants a divorce, it is enough to announce it in the Ispolkom. The other of the spouses is then informed about the divorce having taken place." [9]

In other words, if one party wishes a divorce, it is an injury rather than a benefit to deny it. Continuance of marital relationships, then, should depend upon spontaneity and not compulsion. Marriages which continue even when one of the parties desires discontinuance and separation, or both—as is so frequent in the

[9] "New Law Concerning Marriage, Divorce, Family, and Guardianship," Glikin. (Soviet Pamphlet.)

western world—are but a private madhouse for the individual or individuals. That coercion is an unhealthful and foolish method to be used in marital relations, no progressive thinker would dispute. Marital felicity certainly cannot depend upon legal enforcements. In reference to divorce and coercion, the comment of the Soviet writer Rostovsky is instructive:

"To give any explanations why one of the spouses wants a divorce is unnecessary . . . for to remain married, or to dissolve the marriage, depends entirely upon the desire of one of the spouses; to endeavor to coerce them is impossible, and, therefore, any explanation is unnecessary." [10]

To expedite the simplicity of this process it is not even necessary that the parties desiring divorce appear originally in person:

"A petition for the dissolution of marriage may be presented orally or in writing and an official report shall be drawn thereon."

Shortly thereafter the court will

"set the day for the examination of the petitions and give notice thereof to the parties and (where necessary) their attorneys."

While in the recent agitation in reference to the ex-

[10] Rostovsky, "New Law Concerning Marriage, Family and Guardianship." (Third Edition. Soviet Pamphlet.)

pediency of equalizing registered and unregistered marriages, there was a fervor and fury in the clash of pros and cons, and differences waxed intense and vehement, in the question of divorce there were no pros and cons, in fact, no argument at all. I. I. Iliynski, in reporting the recent conference, declared that "the great majority agreed that the freedom to destroy marriage should be preserved in full."

In the problem of children it is the mother and child that are primarily protected. The presence of children is the only impediment to freedom of divorce. Under these conditions a divorce is not granted until the wife and children have been duly provided for against suffering and deprivation. The husband thus seeking a divorce must apportion his wages according to the decision of the court before the divorce is granted. Under ordinary circumstances, one-third of his wage is requisite for each child. Of course, where there are more than two children, or where his wife is incapacitated for work, other provisions, determined by the case, are made. It can be appreciated at once, from these facts that the *woman and child are consequently saved from suffering and distress.*

Although divorce has now been made open for all, and its pursuit unaccompanied by difficulty of explanation or expenditure, the rate of divorce in Soviet Russia has not been spectacular. The only time when divorces raced beyond normal predictions was at the very beginning of the new code. When the code was first put into effect, it gave an opportunity to thousands who had been oppressed under the marital regulations of the Tzarist régime to take advantage of the new freedom of divorce. Since then the rate has not experienced such exaggerated rations. In 1922, for instance, there were ten divorces for each ten thousand inhabitants; in 1923 there were eleven; and in 1924 and 1925 approximately the same rate persisted. Fifty-three per cent of the divorcees, it should be remarked, had been married for one year, and thirteen per cent for periods of longer duration. When we recall from our previous studies in divorce ratios that the *average in the United States is 15.3 divorces for every ten thousand inhabitants,* the statistics in Soviet Russia might appear comforting even to the conservative. With freedom of divorce the ratio of divorces is less than with the lack of freedom—such an argument might be projected by a moralist from these statistics. It would be unfair, however, not to observe certain factors in the Russian situation that are bound to hold the divorce rate at a surprisingly low level. The practice of unregistered marriages would obviously not affect the divorce rate by virtue of their discontinuance. There would be no record of these separations to enter upon the divorce calendar. It would only be the presence of children that would ever bring them up for social study or consideration. In addition it is very likely, despite the wide discussion of the topic all over Russia, that many peasants do not realize fully the opportunities for individual freedom from marital bondage that is inherent in the new code. The presence of these factors, however, should offer no cause for perturbation or alarm. Increase in divorce is a source of destruction only where the perpetuation of the old family is desired. Divorce in the west is a cancerous evil because it signifies the disintegration of the monogamous family which is still entertained as a moral ideal in both western Europe and the United States. In Soviet Russia where this ideal is contemned as obsolescent, and the future is conceived in terms of its extinction, divorce is a benefit and not an evil.

As the hurly-burly of the young days and months of the Revolution subsided into a more orderly change, ideas and impulses once topsy-turvied by the excitement and drama of spreading chaos, became more soundly oriented and crystallized. In those tumultuous-spirited years of revolution, counter-revolution, intervention and famine, moral revolt went mad with iconoclastic fury. Everything of the old order was flung aside with a contempt bred in bitterness. All traces of old forms and conventions, however vestigial or attenuated, were beaten and buried beneath the derisive epithet of "bourgeois." The word "bourgeois" became synonymous with everything ugly, hideous and indescribably repulsive. Converted into "boorzhooy," it became the embodiment of even more contempt and hatred. In mystic verse that wove the march of "The Twelve" into the footprints of the Revolution, Alexander Blok fused a fantasy, inspired by religious fervor, with sneer and scorn for the "boorzhooy"——

> "The boorzhooy, like a hungry mongrel,
>   A silent question stands and begs,
> The old world like a kinless mongrel
>   Stands there, its tail between its legs."

Youths flaunted with riotous audacity the banners of their revolt. Girls who endeavored to retain the old virtues, or insisted upon delicate discriminations were spurned with ridicule. Students flashed manifestos upon the walls of schools and colleges; chastity was belittled in quip and epigram, and continence was condemned as insane and ridiculous. Freedom became a fetish, and loveliness was lost in excess. The slow restoration of order inserted the first check upon these impetuosities and indiscriminate enthusiasms. Love and the sex-life which had become enmeshed in the confusions of these hectic years gradually disentangled themselves and fumbled about for new foundations. While the old could not be abided, the new could not afford to sacrifice everything precious merely for the sake of novelty. Sex had to be approached with sanity if it was to be mastered by men at all. And so, as the Revolution matured and the new order shaped itself into a new diaphragm, these early exaggerations and excesses dwindled, and the basis of the new morality, organized about the new code, was begun.

It is this new morality which we find expressed in the independent position of woman, and the new marriage and divorce laws written into the legal code of Soviet Russia. In these changes are manifested the first strides in the direction of a new ethic.

CHAPTER XIV

THE ADVANCED ATTITUDE TOWARD BIRTH CONTROL AND ABORTION

IN no other country in the world save Soviet Russia is birth control an actual and open part of educational program and medical practice. Several countries, as we previously described, have become more liberal in their attitude toward birth control, but their liberality has been limited to clinical advice and aid. Birth control clinics in Holland have been organized upon an extraordinarily sane and sanitary basis; such clinics in England have been noteworthy in their efforts to enlighten patients and public; in Germany and Scandinavia progressive work has also been done in these directions. This progression, however, has been very confined in comparison with the astonishing advance made in this field by the Soviet Union.

That the use of contraceptive devices has had a decisive influence in the decline of birth rates in the western world is now a well accepted fact. The interesting connection between the beginning of the decrease in English births from the time of the famous Bradlaugh trial, which first brought the problem of birth control before the minds of the English people, is pertinent in the study of vital statistics. The struggle in England against suppression of birth control information and materials indicated a concern for the issue that was more than superficial. The response of women in England, as measured by their attendance at birth control clinics and solicitations for advice in the nature and use of contraceptives, and the stand in favor of birth control taken by the women in the trade unions, are convincing evidence of the attitude of women toward the problem. While the accessibility of birth control information is now no longer difficult, at the same time it should not be forgotten it is disseminated chiefly at clinics and in books that too often, on account of expense as well as diction, reach only the educated. Birth control information has spread far more widely through personal suggestion and counsel than in any definite educational manner. This has been frequently unfortunate in effect. Contraceptive practices, as a consequence, have often been without success. Manufacturers have exploited this ignorance, and the public has suffered. Such exploitation, ignorance, and suffering can only be avoided when there is an official attitude upon the part of the state in favor of birth control and instruction in its practice.

In Soviet Russia the official attitude is one that not only approves of birth control, but is also active in scientifizing its practice. The Russians approach the whole matter with an exemplary candor. There is no attempt to obscure contraceptive information, or to limit it to clinic or text. On the other hand, there is a serious and insistent endeavor to acquaint the entire populace with information as to birth control, and combat any misinformation in reference to its nature or application.

It is the duty and not merely the privilege of the doctor, for instance, to instruct the people in this practice. A protocol of the Conference of Obstetricians in Moscow (Nov. 21, 1923) stresses this obligation:

"It is the duty of the obstetrician to teach the female population the use of a harmless contraceptive method, whenever pregnancy is impossible or unwanted at the time by the given person."

In general education this same attitude prevails. No distinction is made between married or unmarried women or the existence of merely voluntary choice in the matter or of physical necessity—instruction is given, then, solely because of the desire of the individual to possess it. There is no third degree examination of genealogy, or measurement of preference. Every one possesses this same privilege. It is an official attitude. As a result, men and women in Soviet Russia can be edified in the nature of contraceptive technique in a way that is healthful and scientific. In America, for instance, this same edification can be acquired, but in a way that is clandestine, unchecked and dubious. In the final analysis, in our present age, it is not the dissemination of birth control methods that is at stake —the dissemination occurs, particularly among youth, regardless of law—but the method of dissemination. In America the method must be illegal; hence it suffers from secrecies, inaccuracies and a procedure that is haphazard and precarious. In Soviet Russia the method is legal; hence it is open, accurate and scientific.

The application of the American method of concealment and suppression has dangerous and drastic consequences. As R. L. Dickinson, at the seventy-eighth session of the American Medical Association, stated, the result of this attitude is to "drive the subject of birth control to propaganda organizations." [1] These organizations often deceive the public, as in England, or at best they may frequently prefer a certain type

[1] Discussion of Papers on Maternity Health, Post Natal Care, etc.

of contraceptive that, upon more objective and extensive analysis, might be found to be less effective than another. Certain birth control organizations, of course, although propagandistic in program, endeavor to attain a high degree of scientific accuracy. These organizations, such as the American Birth Control League, sincerely strive to edify and not to exploit the people. Other organizations lack this lofty ethic. In Soviet Russia such tendencies cannot grow.

One of the ways in which the population is taught to appreciate the wisdom of birth control and the methods of its practice, is by generous application of pamphlets on this theme. These pamphlets appear only under state sanction, and, therefore, are guaranteed as to their accuracy and caution. Such pamphlets are sold in thousands of stores and railroad stations at a price that the poorest proletarian or peasant can easily afford. One pamphlet, for instance, that I bought for twenty kopecks at a small railroad station near Moscow, written by Dr. Shpak, entitled "Prevention of Conception" will illustrate the value of this literature. In a section devoted particularly to peasant women, the individual is advised to seek the counsel of a doctor in order to find out which particular contraceptive method would most satisfactorily suit her case. She is specifically warned against certain deleterious methods that are frequent still in the United States and Europe and were practiced in pre-Revolutionary Russia. She is admonished also against many common delusions which have grown up in connection with the avoidance of conception. She is advised "not to be ashamed to talk to a doctor . . . because no doctor can refuse to give advice to a woman, and help her with his knowledge." The sexual organs of both sexes are described in detail in order to acquaint the reader with the scientific differences in anatomy that distinguish male from female, and also to instruct her in a sane and intelligent attitude toward love and the sex-life. Every contraceptive method that is known is considered and analyzed. The dangers attached to the use of certain types are stressed and the advantages associated with others are included in the treatment of the topic. The entire approach is clean and circumspect. The style in which the pamphlet is written is persuasively simple and unconfusing. In itself it is a scientific consideration of the problem expressed in untechnical language.

This attitude toward birth control is intimately connected with the new attitude toward abortion. Abortion is a world menace. The pain and death which it has caused, as we saw in an earlier chapter, are enormous. In order to obviate the great necessity for abortions, instruction in contraceptives is the best preventive. Women who wish to have abortions performed are in most cases women who did not originally anticipate or desire pregnancy. To diminish such cases, the most direct method to be used is that of contraception.

"Abortion is the greatest national menace of our time, and we must struggle with it in every possible way. It is the duty of every physician to aid women to limit and control the birth of children not by way of abortion, but by way of sanitary enlightenment in the application of harmless contraceptives against pregnancy." [2]

This excerpt, quoted from the pamphlet of Dr. Shpak, is typical of the attitude toward abortion that exists today in Soviet Russia. The attempts of misguided and ofttimes malicious interpreters to prove that abortions are advocated in Soviet Russia are false and preposterous.

Although Soviet Russia wishes to discourage abortion, it has not allowed a wish to be mistaken for a fulfillment. Abortions may be attacked, but they do not, therefore, cease. The struggle with abortion in the West, as we have emphasized in our previous chapter on this theme, has been a pronounced and bitter failure. Even when the death penalty had been meted

[2] Dr. H. Z. Shpak, "Prevention of Conception." (Soviet Pamphlet.)

out for the abortionist, the practice had not abated. In the last few generations, it has multiplied in terrifying proportions. The 80,000 criminal abortions which, it will be recalled, it was estimated were effected in New York in one year, denotes something of the extensity of the practice. The toll in death and disease has been appalling. This toll has been largely the result of the illegalization of abortion. Under this illegalization those seeking abortions have had to address the charlatan for aid. The necessity for secrecy, the absence of sanitary, scientific technique and the excellent facilities of a hospital, have been the direct causes for the high mortality resulting from the operation. All these factors, which we have previously described in more detail, were considered by the Soviet authorities before they passed the new law legalizing abortion.

In Tzarist Russia abortions had been increasingly numerous. They had been performed in concealed places by incompetent midwives and quacks. The mortality at times had been even higher than in any country of Europe or the United States. The legalization of abortion elevated the entire operation to another sphere. It destroyed the need for the midwife and quack, and immediately changed the mortality toll.

In a very clear and cogent way S. A. Protoklitov describes the attitude of Soviet Russia:

"Under the Tzarist Government the woman was forced to give birth to children under fear of punishment. But what was the result? Women performed abortions secretly. In cities they turned to private doctors and midwives, in villages to quacks. The Soviet Government decided that this was dangerous and six years ago it issued a special law concerning abortion. According to this law every woman has the right to have an abortion. There is no punishment for this. She has a right to have an abortion in a hospital without any charge at all. *But only a doctor can perform the operation, and the operation can only be performed in a hospital.*" [3]

In another place in this same pamphlet the author explains why the Soviet Government passed the law:

"Why did the Soviet Government issue this law? Does it desire to have a great number of abortions? No, of course not! . . . The Soviet Government wants to approach the problem in a different way from the rest of the world. It wants to destroy the causes which make women desire abortion (by education and the use of contraceptives) . . . but it knows that it is impossible to eradicate these causes at once. Therefore, the Government desires that if a woman cannot do without an abortion she should

[3] "What Peasant Women Should Know about Abortion." By S. A. Protoklitov. (Soviet Pamphlet.)

have it effected in the most sanitary and effective manner. This is only possible when the abortion is done in a hospital and by a doctor." [4]

The exact formulation of the Soviet stand in reference to abortions is to be discovered in the following mandate issued by the Commissariat of Public Health in 1920:

1. Operative interruptions of pregnancy without charge are permitted in the hospitals of the Soviet Government.

2. The performance of such an operation by anyone other than a physician is most strictly prohibited.

3. The midwife or nurse who shall perform such an operation shall be deprived of the right to practice her calling and shall be turned over to the courts for trial.

4. The physician who performs such an operation in his private practice for motives of gain shall be handed over to the trial court.

In 1924 when the demand for abortions began to exceed the capacity of the hospitals to undertake them, the following regulations were established in order to determine in which cases abortions should be effected:

1. Single women out of work who are supported by the labor exchange.

2. Single women, employed, who already have one child.

[4] *Ibid.*

[277]

3. Women employed in the industries, who have several children.

4. Wives of workingmen with several children.

5. All the remaining members of the health insurance societies, and, then, women who are not members of any health insurance society at all.

That it can be said without overstatement that in its decision in reference to abortion Soviet Russia has made the most remarkable and intelligent advance in modern morality, is proven by the results that have accrued from its action. Despite the legalization of abortion a large percentage of women, either unaware of the new law or frightened with terror at the thought of confinement in a hospital (which for many peasant women is still a shockingly new and fearful thing), resorted to "bunglere" for abortions. In the three years 1922, 1923, and 1924, 66,675 of such cases were detected with a mortality of over 3,000. With the spread of education, the destruction of ignorant fears and the eradication of the quack, such cases will necessarily diminish and then disappear. The overwhelming achievement of the new law is to be found in the record of legal abortions accomplished during these three years. As we cited in an earlier chapter, during this period there were 55,320 legal abortions performed,

without the occurrence of a single death.[5] This is
without question a gigantic success. Its significance
can scarcely be exaggerated.

Naturally, the sweep of education and the use of
contraceptives, and their increasing effectiveness in application will prove to be the most intelligent way in
which to combat the need for abortions. The improvement in economic life, it is true, is also important in
that it will prevent children from becoming an economic burden and handicap. The eradication of all
distinction between married and unmarried mothers
will largely destroy the moral motivation for abortion.
In the meanwhile, however, while the demand for abortion still persists, the legalization method of Soviet
Russia is the only sane way in which the evils inevitable in its illegal practice can be eliminated.

[5] Report by Dr. A. B. Genns, Statistician to the Department of
Maternal and Infant Welfare, under Dr. Vera Lebedeva. Quoted
from *Journal of American Medical Association,* December 10, 1927.
Page 2014.

CHAPTER XV

PROSTITUTION AND VENEREAL DISEASE

I N Tzarist Russia prostitution was a plague. The "yellow ticket" effected no better protection than the "passports" in Paris and Berlin. Houses of prostitution were often opened officially by the state, with the blessing of the priest as part of the inaugural procedure. Since the Revolution, prostitution has been made illegal. Prostitution, however, has not ceased. Those who romanticize about the disappearance of prostitution in Soviet Russia adopt a sophomoric outlook. Until the entire economic conditions in Soviet Russia can be changed, and poverty totally destroyed, it will be impossible to exterminate the practice. At the same time, the methods employed by Soviet Russia to prevent its increase and expansion, have been characterized by an intelligence that is without parallel in the approach to the same task by other nations. The means of curbing and combating prostitution in other countries have been pitifully childish and futile. Even these means, as in America, have more often been taken by societies of crusading moralists rather than by the state. The method of "dispersal" through destruction of "common centers," has been most frequently utilized. Destruction of "red light districts," it is thought, will destroy the evils of prostitution. Few conclusions are so essentially foolish as this. The results have always confirmed its folly. The method of control through "passports" or registration cards, has likewise proven of little aid. Even as a protective against venereal infection this latter method has been a deplorable failure. Only in Soviet Russia has there been no trifling with mere effects without regard for their causes. The measures enacted in an attempt to diminish the evil have always been of a type devised to check the cause.

One of the main problems, in the struggle with prostitution, as we stated in the report published in the Izvestia (of the Central Ispolkom, Nov. 11, 1926), is that involved in the battle with the brothel-keepers. In thirty states in one year 704 houses of prostitution were opened, 264 in state cities, 159 in cities, and 281 in country locations. The cities most deeply infested with this menace are, in order of seriousness, Moscow, Leningrad, Samara, and Stalingrad.[1] This report was

[1] It should be understood that it is those who encourage or profit by prostitution who are punished instead of the prostitute herself, unless she can be definitely shown to have spread venereal disease in the practice of her vocation.

made by Kiselev, the chief of the militia. It is what has been done to eradicate this evil which is important. In the first place, the problem has been subjected to profound investigation and study. One of the first facts discovered was that the unemployment of single women was one of the greatest dangers. Over 32% of the prostitutes in Moscow, for instance, are by occupation house-workers (Izvestia, Nov. 11, 1926). Consequently, a resolution has been passed which declares that, in the event of unemployment, "single women should be 'laid off' last. Such an advance in social therapeutics is of epoch-making character. No country has ever officially tackled this problem in such a causal manner. No country has ever made such an endeavor to control economic life in a struggle against social evils. As an instance of the interest that the people have as a whole taken in the problem of prostitution, we find considerations of the topic, recommendations and admonitions in many trade-union newspapers, wall-newspapers, and periodicals. It was the workingwomen of the confectionery shop, entitled Red October, that first addressed the Moscow Soviet with the following recommendation:

"Don't lay off single workingwomen and then prostitution will decrease."

The workingwomen in the factory Red Confectioner

and in the confectionery shop Bolshevik also urged strict surveillance by the militia of the bath houses and hotels which had become "nests of prostitution." [2] Semashka, Commissar of Public Health, also pointed out in this same connection the growth of prostitution in the Sandunovski and Central Bath Houses. It was claimed that during two hours of observation fifty prostitutes were detected in the Sandunovski Baths. A suggestion to close the baths as places tending to increase prostitution was acted upon by the Soviet and its recommendation placed before the presidium of the Moscow Soviets.

One of the best ways to struggle with prostitution was found to be the organization of homes for unemployed women. In Moscow these homes have become a great aid in the struggle. These homes, organized by the Union of Public Health, supply places where women out of work can sleep at nights. This also is a wonderfully intelligent social tactic. Many other homes have been organized purely for the reformation of prostitutes. These homes give the prostitute shelter and food, and above all, strive to teach her a trade. This is an economic way of fighting an economic evil. In this way, the economic factor has a direct influence in the moral equation. Bogdanov, representing the

[2] *Working Paper*, January 25, 1927. Page 5.

Trade Union of Public Nutrition, has been active in the creation of more homes for unemployed domestic workers. A project has also been worked out by the Union of Public Health to organize "with a labor régime for three thousand incorrigible prostitutes." In every manner, then, prostitution has been attacked not by dispersal but by weakening its economic motivations.

As a result of these measures and methods, H. A. Semashko, reports that prostitution has distinctly decreased. It is now less than in the pre-War period.

One of the striking evidences given by Semashko for the decrease in prostitution in Soviet Russia, is the decline in percentage of venereal infections contracted from prostitutes which is to be noted at the present time. Syphilis and gonorrhea have found in prostitution their chief medium of dissemination. That venereal diseases have outleaped all other diseases, and even superseded tuberculosis, as the most frequent and fatal of human ills, can be accounted for chiefly on the basis of the spread of prostitution and the failure to institute adequate treatment in prophylactics.[3]

[3] In order to point out the spread of these infections the disease statistics of any country will suffice. Approximately 1,000,000 cases (999,351 to be exact) of gonorrhea were reported in the United States in the last six years. (*Albany Health News*, Albany, 1927—IV, 75.) In 1925, 39 states in the United States reported 206,566 cases of

Our contention is not that prostitution in itself explains this phenomenal rise in venereal disease, but that the growth of prostitution is one of the important factors that expedited the increase, and that it is also one of the most important influences in retarding its diminution. The incidence of venereal infections among prostitutes, as would be expected, has always

syphilis among a population of 1,875,000. (*Public Health Reports,* January 7, 1927. XLII, No. 1, Treasury Department, Washington, D. C.) It is the opinion of gynecologists in the United States at least, that gonorrhea if not syphilis has become endemic. According to Morrow, 60% of the adult male population of the United States have gonorrhea. In Czecho-Slovakia in 1921 more than 21,000 cases were reported. The multiplication of venereal infections in Rumania had become so alarming that a campaign was recently projected to raise 1,000,000 lei to fight any further distribution of these diseases. In the Italian army in 1922, for instance, 11,700 men suffered from these infections. In other armies the figures are not more comforting. The War which aided prostitution, doubled, tripled and quadrupled venereal attacks, despite introduction of prophylactic stations, and enforced prophylactic treatments for all soldiers who had sexual relations. During the year of 1919 solely, men in the British army lost approximately 2,000,000 days from duty as a result of venereal diseases. ("The Campaign against Venereal Disease in Great Britain," Mrs. Neville Rolfes. *World's Health,* Paris, 1925.) In the American army, even in the comparatively brief time in which the American soldiers were in Europe, gonorrhea alone caused a loss of 127,018 days. (*Journal of American Medical Association,* December 31, 1927.) In France the figures are spectacular. No matter where we glance the ravages wrought by these diseases are far-stretching and horrible. (The decrease of incidence of recent syphilis, in answer to a questionnaire replied to by fourteen countries is scarcely a source of much hope, since the statistics of pre-war incidence were not included in the questionnaire.)

been exceedingly high. Among 533 prostitutes examined by Huber, 59.6% had gonorrhea. Among 407 prostitutes observed by Prowe, gonorrhea was present in 76.6% of the cases. These statistics, one must realize, are gathered only from those prostitutes who through illness became available for examination and study. If all prostitutes could be examined the percentage infected would no doubt be immediately augmented. As a consequence of this high degree of infection and when considered in connection with the dismaying frequency with which sex contacts are effected in this trade, the prepotent part that prostitution plays in spreading venereal disease can easily be appreciated.

There are only three ways to stem the increase in venereal ills, and they are to inaugurate a physical examination of the populace in order to treat congenital or incipient cases before they become active and dangerous; establish sufficient prophylactic hospitals and stations to treat cases immediately after contacts suspect to the individuals; and sharply check, in an endeavor to eventually eliminate prostitution. The institution of such prophylactic treatment in the Italian army for example, reduced the number of men contracting venereal infection from 11,700 in 1922 to 5,040 in 1925. Such prophylactic treatment, however, can be successful only when a general educational program is carried on in support of it. The situation in France already has become so alarming, in fact, almost beyond control, that such a program, in an indefinite way, has already been started. Moving pictures have even been used as a form of propaganda to attack venereal disease. Two well-known moving pictures of this kind that had been frequently thrown upon the screen in Paris are *Syphilis, a Social Scourge,* and *Social Hygiene in Woman.* In 1926, 9,650,000 francs were appropriated for the control of venereal disease. There are now 395 anti-syphilitic dispensaries. Nevertheless prostitution is combatted in ways that can only result in failure. The method of regulation by "passports" has been generally pursued. The futility of this method has long ago been recognized. The statement of the British Social Hygiene Council is conclusive:

"The regulation of prostitution has not at any time or in any country helped to limit the damages caused by venereal infection."

It is only in Soviet Russia that the problem of venereal disease has been met with in connection with its intimate relationship to prostitution. Prostitution, as we described, has been met there not by vain triflings with its surface-manifestations but by grappling with its actual causation. Baths are closed, as we have seen, when they are found to encourage prostitution, and every effort is made to study specifically those localities and those economic situations which tend to heighten this menace. Compulsory examination and treatment for those infected with venereal disease is implied in the new article in the penal code. The decision of the All-Russian Central Committee in reference to measures used to exterminate venereal disease is further evidence of a far-sighted social tactic. Individuals are responsible to the court not only for infecting others with venereal disease but also those are responsible who expose others to the danger of infection. Information as to prophylactics is widely distributed as part of sex education and the practice of social hygiene. It is not surprising therefore, that Semashko reports, as we stated before, that venereal infection from prostitutes has decreased in Soviet Russia and that more recent figures indicate that venereal infections over the country as a whole have experienced an emphatic reduction.

CHAPTER XVI

THE FUTURE MORALITY IN SOVIET RUSSIA

"What are we? Bourgeois moralists, that we occupy ourselves with such a distinction?!"

IN these words of Moirova, which we quoted before, is crystallized the challenge of an epoch. This is a new age with idealism hung in the windows of men's souls and not upon the stars. Here is an earnest effort to realize what in the past has burnt in men's minds only as an aspiration. A new life is being forged out by the work of active revolutionary intelligences.

Conflicts in political life may disconcert and even dismay, obstacles in economic evolution may retard and even necessitate temporary retreat, but the organization of a new order, the creation of a new outlook, the conception of a new morals, have already developed expression and form that can never be converted back into the old. A new generation has grown up under Soviet influence, and this generation reflects this new life. Even a counter-revolution cannot change ideas

[289]

and attitudes which have been nurtured in youth and fortified in maturity by a revolutionary environment.

These men and women in Russia are struggling to realize a new era. This new morality, which we have described and discussed, is as much a part of this new existence as is the new economics which is inherent in its structure. It is a vast revolutionary change, this in Soviet Russia, that leaves no phase of life untouched.

This new moral life which Soviet Russia has endeavored to achieve is new only in social realization for the radical. Far-flung Utopias had conjured it up in spheres remote from reality and sequestered from struggle. Dreamers had visioned it amid the effusions of fancy, and talked of it as a hope winged upon angelic transformations. Revolutionaries had outlined its practicality in a world emancipated from economic conflict. The manumission of women was foretold as the first step. This in itself, if the manumission were moral as well as economic and political, would have occasioned a revolution in ethics.

In Soviet Russia, while conditions are still transitionary, and the change to the new order is far from complete, the advance toward the revolutionary ideals entertained by the radical has been exceptionally rapid. Woman has been freed, as we have seen, and the old morality and conventions, based upon a property concept, have been mainly discarded. While certain old forms are still retained this is only because the total transformation of society has not yet been consummated.

Bebel's description of the new society is no longer confined to the dubious promise of prophecy:

"In the new society woman will be entirely independent, both socially and economically. She will not be subjected to even a trace of domination and exploitation, but will be free and man's equal and mistress of her own lot.

"In the choice of love she is as free and unhampered as man. She woos or is wooed, and enters into a union prompted by no other considerations than her own feelings. The union is a private agreement, without the interference of a functionary, just as marriage had been a private agreement until far into the Middle Ages. Here socialism will create nothing new; it will merely reinstate on a higher level of civilization and under a different social form what generally prevailed before private property dominated society.

"Man shall dispose of his own person, provided that the gratification of the impulses is not harmful or detrimental to others. The satisfaction of the sexual impulse is as much the private concern of such individual as the satisfaction of any other natural impulse. No one is accountable to anyone else, and no third person has a right to interfere. What I eat and drink, how I sleep and dress, is my own private affair, and my private affair also is my intercourse with a person of the opposite sex." [1]

This situation has already been partly realized in Soviet Russia. This new independent woman in Russia has become "man's equal and mistress of her own lot."

All over the industrial world, the United States, England, Germany, France, the family has experienced, as we have shown, an endless series of devastating shocks and titubations. It has disintegrated beyond repair. Nevertheless there is a fear in these countries to admit this fact and face the future that, in terms of their norm, is growing more and more ominous. The new morality for them is the new destruction. In Soviet Russia the breakdown of the family is not a regret and the rise of the new morality not an evil.

That "the monogamous family must cease to be the industrial unit of society . . . with the emancipation of women" was stressed by Engels years ago.[2] Belfort Bax was even more definite in his vaticinatory declarations:

"There are few points on which the advanced radical and the socialist are more completely in accord than in their

[1] "Woman and Socialism." Bebel.
[2] "Origin of the Family," page 90.

theoretic hostility to the modern legal monogamic marriage. The majority of them hold it, even at the present time, and in the existing state of society, to be an evil. . . .

"Socialism will strike at the root at once of compulsory monogamy and prostitution by inaugurating an era of marriage based on free choice and intention and characterized by no external coercion."

Others than revolutionary radicals recognized the necessary truth of these pronunciamentos and predictions. H. G. Wells, in discussing the future of the family, asserted:

"Essentially the socialist position is a denial of property in human beings . . . women and children, just as much as men and things, must cease to be chattels. Socialism indeed proposes to abolish altogether the patriarchal family amidst whose disintegrating ruins we live and to raise women to equal citizenship with men." [3]

W. L. George was equally direct:

"The ultimate aim of Feminism with regard to marriage is the practical suppression of marriage and the institution of free alliance." [4]

Edward Carpenter, another English thinker, in urging a new moral order, indicted the bourgeois family be-

[3] "Socialism and the Family."
[4] "Feminist Intentions," *Atlantic Monthly*. Vol. 2, No. 6.

cause it carried with it "an odious sense of stuffiness and narrowness, moral and intellectual." In another place he stated "that the type of family which it provides is too often like that which is disclosed when, on turning over a large stone, we disturb an insect Home that seldom sees the light." [5]

In the work of Kollontai we have the Bolshevik attitude toward sex and family life very clearly projected. Her words are not splintered with evasions:

"It is necessary to declare the truth outright, the old form of the family is passing away; the communist society has no use for it. The bourgeois world celebrated the isolation, the cutting off of the married pair from the collective weal; in the scattered and disjointed individual bourgeois society, full of struggle and destruction, the family was the sole anchor of hope in the storms of life, the peaceful haven in the ocean of hostilities and competitions between persons. The family represented an independent class in the collective unit. There can and must be no such thing in the communist society. For communist society as a whole represents such a fortress of the collective life, precluding any possibility of the existence of an isolated class of family bodies, existing by itself, with its ties of birth, with its love of family honor, its absolute segregation.

"Already ties of blood, of birth, and even of the relationship of conjugal love, are weakening in our eyes; in their

[5] Carpenter's "Love's Coming of Age."

[294]

turn are growing, spreading, and deepening, new ties, ties of the working family, the profound feeling of comradeship, of solidarity, of community of interests, the creation of a collective responsibility, of a belief in the collective welfare as the highest moral-legislative good."

Here we see the passing of the family regarded without reluctance or lament. In truth, it is welcomed. Modern monogamy has been a static relationship at basis. While it originally expressed something of the fixity of feudalism, and as a fiction functioned in the matter of the inheritance of feudal estates and pre-rogatives, it should be remembered, that, as Calhoun suggested, it arose "apparently from the 'lower' classes where economic conditions forbade polygamic connections." Monogamy is a social institution that expresses a social age. Its original economic justification is apparent. It extols the family instead of the group. It exalts family pleasures instead of communal. An illustration of this fact is to be discovered in the attitude of the Protestant Reformers who denounced all communal pleasures as derivative of the decay of the Catholic Church. During the Middle Ages, it should be noted, life was comparatively communal in its economic endeavors as well as in its diversions and delights. It was the coming of the commercial revolution, and, rising upon it on machine-made

[295]

stilts, the Industrial, that brought modern individualistic society into being. This individualistic society, as our previous comments have emphasized, scorned this earlier life and erected in modern monogamy and the modern family a closed-in moral pattern of existence. Modern monogamy, thus, is a result of this set of economic conditions and relations. In its fundamental aspect, monogamy always represents the evolution of the property concept. In the western world monogamy has invariably been associated with the subordination and subjection of woman. All the exaltation of the pure and simple mother, the sweet, domestic wife, has been nothing more than social subterfuge, a euphemism protective to the social status of man. At the same time that woman's domestic function was exalted, she was bartered and sold in market and street. Her education was discouraged, her individuality thwarted, her political rights denied, her property possessions curtailed. Wherever we turn, in primitive times, ancient history or the modern world, the existence of monogamy has meant the enslavement of women. It has meant also the supremacy of the property ideal.

Side by side with monogamy have flourished concubinage and prostitution. The attitude of Cato who declared that "the husband is the judge of his wife, if she has committed a fault he punishes her; if she has drunk wine he condemns her; if she has committed adultery he kills her"; is not guilty of greater tyranny than the actions of the English and Germans who sold their wives and children. The Saxon law of the ninth century which fixed the price of woman at three hundred shillings was scarcely an improvement over the Grecian ideal as voiced by Demosthenes:

"We marry women to have legitimate children and to have faithful guardians of our homes; we maintain concubines for our daily service and comfort; and courtesans for the enjoyment of love."

Woman in the industrial era, as we now know, fared little better until economic independence could inform her revolt with confidence and courage. This very economic independence, however, undermined the family. The necessities of this new life attracted her from the home instead of to it. The family, therefore, weakened and decayed.

Kollontai's opposition to the family is founded upon the clash between individualistic and social ideals. The family was destructively individualistic in its influence. It built its life around a little group instead of the entire community. Affections, hatreds, fears, aspirations were so focussed within these narrow family precincts that social feelings altogether withered. Deep emotions were only felt for those within one's own immediate group and not for men and women in the mass. While in the Middle Ages the wealthy were scorned if they did not give to the poor and usury was condemned by Church and State, the individualistic age forgot everything humanitarian in its mad struggle for money and profits. Through inheritance and through association, individual families were favored and exalted. The suffering of countless millions in factory and mill meant little to those living upon these labors, provided their own families were unharmed. This restriction of interests and sympathies has created an anti-social reaction. It is this anti-social reaction which Kollontai wants to eradicate from life. The disappearance of bourgeois monogamy will remove these family restrictions, and open up the possibilities for the growth of social emotions in a more communal life. Men and women will have affections that will become expansive and not ingrown. Sorrows will not be limited to a small group, nor pleasures shared in clannish form. Social sympathy will supersede family avarice.

With this change, which is only in its incipiency in Soviet Russia, the new attitude toward love and the sex-life that has developed was inevitable. Kollontai's words are of significance not because they voice her opinions as an individual, but because they are expressed in the very nature of the new mores.[6] That there is no fear of ephemereal relations or alliances of brief duration is obvious from another of her declarations:

"Can the short duration, the informality, the freedom of the relation between the sexes be regarded, from the standpoint of working humanity, as a crime, as an act that should be subject to punishment? Of course not. The freedom of relation between the sexes does not contradict the ideology of communism. The interests of the commonwealth of the workers are not in any way disturbed by the fact that marriage is of a short or a long duration, whether its basis is love, passion, or even a transient physical attraction.

"The only thing that is harmful to the workers' collective state and therefore inadmissible, is the element of material

[6] While a number of the older Bolsheviks such as Riazanov and Lunacharsky are opposed to the sweeping sentiments of Kollontai, and lean somewhat toward a communistic puritanism, the disagreement is really one of immediacy and not of fundament. Kollontai strikes them as too brash and precocious in her declarations. They are more timid and cautious in their predictions. They consider the family very necessary during the transitionary era. To what degree their timidity is a matter of age, as has been interestingly suggested, it is difficult to assert. Nevertheless, the people in their daily lives are not turning toward puritanism as an ideal. And furthermore, the very nature of the new marital code, and the destruction of all differences between registered and unregistered marriages, fortify Kollontai's position rather than that of her opponents.

calculation between the sexes, whether it be in the form of prostitution, in the form of legal marriage—the substitution of a crassly materialistic calculation of gain for a free association of the sexes on the basis of mutual attraction."

The very conception of monogamy presumes a certain longevity if not permanence of affection. Although this ideal of monogamy may have been exquisite inspiration to the Victorian poet, it is but idle evasion to the contemporary psychologist. That magnetism which we have been in the habit of describing as love is beautiful but brief. Its very electricity springs from the sexual impulse. The excitement of sex attraction gives it spirit and momentum. Although it may be maintained that this is not all of the love experience, it must be admitted, without referring to Freud, that it is its basis. The excitement disappears with the repeated realization of the sex desire. Tentatively at least it may even be stated as a psychological law that, with constancy of contact, the enjoyment of sex-relationship decreases in inverse ratio to its repetition. The thrill of discovery disappears, and what once was golden glow fails even to glitter. With this inevitable change, passion dims and love fades either into indifference, dislike or devotion. The exhilaration which we have called romance, however, is irretrievably lost. This is a fact which practically every psychologist has known, but has been unwilling to declare. The layman proves it by action and proverb. With woman, due to cultural influence, no doubt more than to any other factor, the experience often is not similar, and it is this disparity in reaction that is additional cause of difficulty and conflict.

In the past the significance of the love-emotion has been either obscured or neglected. Yet its potency as the inspiration if not origin of art can be detected in the recurrence of the erotic motif in artistic substance. With institutionalized monogamy the galvanic impulse of sex is fettered. Few active, sensitive minds submit to it. The notorious immorality of the artist is an expression of this revolt. Sublimation, always a dubious deflection of desire, is not often a satisfactory solution. Change, variety, newness, seem to be part of the ineluctable demands of the sexual impulse. Through cultural inhibitions the feminine impulse has taken on a monogamous character that will undoubtedly disappear with the new morality of the next epoch.

Of course, it should be remembered, in sex-relationships tastes differ as they do toward food and drink. All are necessary, but some prefer one type and others prefer another. Some may unquestionably desire lifelong monogamy; many may abhor it. Its advantages in the new age, the threshold of which we have already crossed, as we have pointed out, are not such as to elicit wide enthusiasm. The change of economic system and social environment alone have rendered monogamy a struggling fiction. It is part of an old age. It cannot be the marital basis of the new. The direction of economic life, and the drive of sexual impulse, are in revolt against it.

What has happened in Soviet Russia represents only the vanguard of this change. Already in the rest of the world this new moral attitude has risen in formidable protest against the old. The revolt of youth, the rise of the new woman and the new morality, and the decay of marriage, are but a few of its early manifestations. Its eventual success is dependent merely upon the speed of time and circumstance.

AN EPILOGUE

CHAPTER XVII

LOVE AND THE SEX LIFE

I

Now that we have considered the general chaos of our era, the decline of an old morality and an old marriage order, and described the forms of revolt which have arisen out of the confusions of decay, we are in a position to discuss the problems of love and the sex life, without the embarrassing inhibitions and timidities of a confined and rigorous ethic. That our conclusions cannot escape the conditioning forces and factors active in the contemporary world is a limitation, of course, that we are cognizant of without argument. All logic, after all, in one form or another, is socio-logic—and then psycho-logic—(The influence of class-mores, for instance, can only be finally escaped when there are no more classes.) A world catastrophe might break upon us in such shattering form that all ideas as to moral reorganization might shift into entirely different directions and defy present predictions. This, to be sure, is unlikely.

In the revolutionary attitude of Soviet Russia, we find an attempt to escape from the ethics of a decadent social class, and construct an ethic that will eventually be the ethic of a classless society. The presence of social classes still in Soviet Russia, of course, handicaps the final development of this ethic. Nevertheless, an advance has been made there toward this ideal which is of significance in the evolution of modern morals.

In these concluding pages, therefore, we shall try to consider changes in terms of their final emancipation from class-influence and class-bias. Only in this way can we arrive at conclusions of meaning or value.

2

Sex has always been an important element in the life of man. Many have interpreted it as the most fundamental. Institutions and customs have been explained in terms of their connection with the sexual life. Alterations in social structure have been associated with sexual revolutions. Human progress and aspiration have been accounted for as results of the sexual urge.

Our own age is one in which this sex monism has become prominent. Sex has become an obsession. This is partly a result of the suppression of all considerations of sex during the last few centuries and primarily the result of the changes in objective institutions which have accomplished this emancipation from these earlier silences.

While sex has been one of the most profound forces in human life, it has not determined social change or economic progress. While its potency may have remained a constant down through the eons and ages, its influence upon group advance has been secondary rather than primary, negative rather than positive. To many in the contemporary world who are ardent advocates of sex emancipation this observation may appear disappointingly conservative. Our zeal for change, however, should not cause us to lose our sense of equilibrium. We must not challenge sex stupidities by sex exaggerations. Through climatic changes and economic revolutions man has advanced, and his sex life has altered with the variations in existence which have resulted. His sexual customs have oscillated with the movement of external conditions. They have not determined this movement; this movement, the other hand, has determined them, their form and expression. Sexual ethics, therefore, are more of an effect than a cause in the progress of social relations. They reflect rather than determine the nature of advance.

Although the variations in custom and convention have been intricate and numerous, and sex attitudes have topsied this way and that as conditions and circumstances altered, the sexual impulse itself has been a factor in the determination of their observance and continuity. In other words a convention that utterly disregarded the nature of the sexual impulse could not long endure. A custom, for instance, which endeavored to enforce celibacy upon men as a necessary form of ethical behavior could only induce its own destruction. Either it would modify itself so that adaptation could be made to it, or it would become so evaded in action that its existence would become merely nominal. We can see then, that change in moral custom, while enormous in potentiality, is still limited within a certain radius. The clash between economics and impulse, which we have hitherto pointed out as inescapable in our own system of ethics, had sown within its very substance the seeds of revolt. This revolt, nevertheless, could only have grown to the proportions of a revolution with the changes in conditions that have given it an increasingly wide chance for expression.

If we succeed in nothing else, in these concluding pages, than in stressing the impermanence of sex attitudes, we shall be content. Men have always been deluded by the fiction that whatever is has always been or is the best that could be. This condition of psychological inertia, disturbed only at moments of immediate and commanding crisis, dynamited into action only when life has become insufferable, has impeded all intellectual and moral advance. The morality of our age, or rather the old morality of the past age, which many of us have known, had once seemed a lasting attribute of a great civilization. We have in our own day seen this morality change and decay. The fear which many experience of witnessing the rise of a new morality and a new moral structure is a fear grounded upon individual rationalization and historical ignorance.

With primitive man sex was a superstition, with ancient man it was a religious cult. The primeval attitude toward sex was free of pruriency and secretiveness. The sex organs were symbols of potency and objects of adoration. Even the exanimate world was endowed with sexual attributes. In the primitive concept of the gods was embodied the sexual origin of the world. Uranus (SKY), for example, was the male in unending sexual congress with Gea (EARTH), the female; in this embrace humanity was conceived as in a constant state of propagation. With the Biblical Jews the phallus was a sacred symbol,[1] sworn by in oath, and worn by the women as a charm of fertility. Phallic worship among the Greeks and Romans was a widespread and accepted custom. In all these attitudes

[1] Inman, "Ancient, Pagan and Modern Christian Symbolism."

sex has a social aspect. It is translated into every form of life. In art its manifestations are arresting and signal. The Comedy, for instance, as Aristotle observed, originated in the Phallic performances, in honor of Phales himself. Greek religion is saturated with sex. Judaism likewise embodies the concrete evidences of phallicism. Not only did the Jews swear by the Phallus,[2] according to Biblical testimony, but their sacred oath of calling on Asher, or Baal as witness was another unmistakable trace of phallic worship.[3] Christianity utilized the same phallic technique. Early architecture which had symbolized the male and female organs in its form and structure was employed by Christianity in the design of its churches and cathedrals.[4] The Trinitarian Conception, in ecclesiastical schemata and architectural design, grew into the male and female triangle, forms of which still linger in the symbol used by the Y. M. C. A. and Y. W. C. A. In a hundred forms Christianity continues, in deviations that fail to disguise their origin, this early influence of the sex motif upon its structure.

As late as 1620 we have upon the English stage vestiges of ancient sex worship. In a masque of the

[2] *Ibid.*
[3] O. A. Wall, "Sex and Sex Worship." Page 384.
[4] Inman. Reference 1.

time, published in 1620 by Edward Wright, and entitled "A Courtly Masque: The Device called the World Tost at Tennis," we discover the phallic symbol in marked evidence. In another play of the time *The Alchemist* by Ben Jonson, we discover the people flocking to see a child whose genitalia were excessive if not monstrous in development, and in *Henry VIII* we discover Shakespeare referring to an Indian abnormally large in his sex organs.[5] All through the Restoration period, likewise, this candor in things sexual reigned.

It has only been since the eighteenth and nineteenth centuries, with the rise of the bourgeois class and its narrow-bound morality, as we saw in earlier chapters, that sex became discussion-gagged by the censor. The stork now became the errand boy of the doctor, and ignorance was sweetly cherished as innocence. Candor became a vice, and hypocrisy a virtue. Art in the nude was draped, legs suddenly became limbs, and passion became a sin of the pagans. The difference between the clean attitude of ancient man toward sex and the unclean attitude of modern man is well illustrated in the controversy that arose about the Greek play *Lysistrata*. In this play, when it was originally staged in Greece, the actors wore artificial phalli, and no one was either shocked, surprised or bewildered. When

[5] For further details cf. author's book "Sex Expression in Literature."

Aubrey Beardsley, however, illustrated this Greek play according to its original form, with its phallicism manifest, he horrified the bourgeois world, and was scorned and attacked with unmitigated vigor.

To primitive and ancient man, it is clear, sex was a significant phenomenon, which he approached with reverence and candor. He did not allow the element of shame to intrude into his conception of it. He did not attempt to obscure or deny its realities. He spoke of the organs of procreation with affection and with a clean respect for their potency. To him sex embodied the mysterious source of creation and he idealized it in art and religion. Modern man, on the contrary, has been taught either to look upon sex as a sin, or as something unclean and unbeautiful except in its stupid sentimentalities and childish bathos. He has endeavored to hide it, and confine it to the unspoken. He has encouraged ignorance of it as an ideal. Pruriency and smugness grew up as characteristic manifestations of this ostrich-like attitude. An unclean and unhealthy "refinement" was the consequence. It was not until our present generation that this "refinement" was recognized as a form of hypocrisy, a spurious virtue that brought only ignorance and pain, and a sense of sickening impotency with its realization.

This morality of the modern age, prior to the de-

velopments in the new generation, revolved about a
certain set of ideas embedded in the concept of monogamy. Its ideals of chastity, monogamous fidelity,
and a subjection of the sex life to the demands of
the economic order, were not of long duration. A
great number of people imagine that these sex ideals
are the creation of civilized man, and that all other
sex attitudes were the outgrowths of barbarous and
pagan cultures. They conceive of their approach to
sex as something ultimately pure, the acme of moral
achievement. This belief, of course, is ridiculous, nay
risible. It has no foundation other than the desire
to justify that which one has known and in which one
has faith.

Sexual customs in modern times as well as in ancient
reveal wide and sweeping fluctuations. The concept of
chastity has often been singled out as something which
all moralities have advocated. This again is nothing
more than an attempt to force historical fact to fit one's
moral predilections. It is, of course, essentially fallacious. Among primitive peoples chastity is often considered a vice instead of a virtue. Among the Nasa-
monians the custom is for the bride to surrender herself to all the wedding guests before she welcomes her
husband. Herodotus describes this custom in the following manner:

[313]

"When a Nasamonian marries, it is the custom for the first night to lie with all the guests in turn, and each, when he has intercourse with her, gives her some present which he has brought with him." [6]

Pomponius Mela claimed that greater honor attached to those women who had many such sex relations on their wedding night than those who had but a few. [7] Diodorus, commenting upon the customs of the inhabitants of the Belearic Islands, wrote:

"They have a strange custom at their weddings, for on the wedding night the oldest friends and guests lie first with the bride; then the others in the order of their ages. The bridegroom is the last man who is admitted to that honor." [8]

Even at the present day this same custom continues among the Barea of Abyssinia, the Australian aborigines, and the Waitata and the Watveta of East Africa. Similar usages existed in New Guinea, Cuba, Peru and Central America. Among Southern Slavs, until a short time ago, it was the convention for the two best men at the wedding to spend the night with the bride in bed before she experienced the embrace

Briffault, "The Mothers."
Ibid.
[8] *Ibid.*

of her husband.[9] Until fifty years ago it was still the custom for the male guests to disrobe the bride in the nuptial chamber. Just as it had been the practice in ancient Ireland for the king to deflower every bride before she reached her husband. Fertility in these early societies was important, and not virginity. The fear of hemorrhage accompanying defloration was perhaps the main reason for the contempt for virginity. Virginity is often the source of great superstitious fear. Many peoples, for instance, specifically enjoined early intercourse in order to avoid the stigma of virginity. In Egypt the girl had to lose her virginity by promiscuous intercourse prior to puberty. With the Basoga-Batamba of Uganda virginity in a woman, who has reached a marriageable age, is considered criminal. Among the Bushango the aim of a girl after she has been betrothed is to have frequent intercourse with many men in order to occasion a pregnancy. This is an accomplishment which gratifies her prospective husband because it is definite assurance that she is not sterile. The Indians of Canada were so inbred with the same idea that a pregnant girl was the greatest attraction for men anxious to marry. In the Philippines, the Bisayos scorn their wives if they prove virgins. In Nigeria, among the Kaje, this same attitude predomi-

[9] *Ibid.*

nates. A virgin there can command only the price of a goat; a girl who has already borne a child, however, is worth a horse. In the Congo regions a virgin is worth only one-sixth as much as a woman who has had a child. In New Zealand women are considered fortunate because they have never known when they were virgins—for they have love affairs with boys almost from the cradle. This tendency to unrestricted intercourse from childhood is to be found among most primitive and many ancient peoples. Only in certain places, where virginity is associated with property-value, is this general freedom reined-in by an economic custom. It is a curious phenomenon that virginity should be particularly guarded in parts of Africa where the influence of the slave-trade was most profound.[10] And wherever it is guarded it is done so because of its economic value and not moral virtue.

With the exaltation of virginity is associated the subjection of women. Virginity has a value for the man who sells the woman or who purchases the wife. It is not the woman who profits by the economic asset which her virginity commands—but the man. With the Chinese, for instance, where feminine purity has evolved in its expression such an exaggerated finesse,

[10] For many of these references indebtedness is owed to Briffault's excellent study of old mores in his book "The Mothers."

the woman has known freedom only as an alien concept. While suicide in defense of one's virtue is not
an uncommon gesture on the part of the Chinese
woman, Chinese men indulge in a variety of sexual
freedoms all of which are entirely approved by custom.
Little Wives become their property as well as their
Great Wife; female slaves are often employed to offer
more devious thrills for their master's erotic proclivi-
ties; and the habit of providing prostitutes for the en-
tertainment of male friends is a frequent practice
among the mandarins. It is only the woman who is
forced to protect her purity. Among those peoples in
which women are dominant, we do not find them en-
slaving themselves in any such manner. In fact they
maintain a greater freedom in their sexual relations
often than the men. In Uganda, Hawaii, Tahiti,
Paraguay, Sierra Leone, Madagascar and among the
Bosonge of the Congo, Briffault tells us women disdain
such virtues as foolish and unnatural. In these places
women are not subject to men.

That the propertied aspect of virginity has continued
even in the concepts of modern life is proven by the
differentiation and influence of customs upon various
classes in society. While the middle and upper classes
attached great importance to pre-nuptial chastity and
post-nuptial fidelity, the lower classes regarded them

with much less consideration. The buying and selling of wives, as we have learned, was practiced by them in England even when the virtuous Victorians were delivering their preachments to the English Empire. Among the peasants, particularly in Russia, but also in other parts of Europe, virginity was and is relatively inconsequential. In parts of Holland today it is rare for girls to be virgins after puberty, and an advanced state of pregnancy is often an inducement instead of deterrent to marriage.[11] In many of the rustic districts of Bavaria, Austria, Norway and Switzerland, even the presence of illegitimate children is not considered a handicap for a woman who wishes to marry. In a village near Lisbon, virginity is scorned:

"Young girls who reach the age of about sixteen and are still virgins are the object of so much ridicule that in order to avoid the shame they yield themselves with the greatest. readiness to the first man who courts their favors and those ephemeral and unmoral unions continue until the girl is pregnant. Then a new life begins for her. He who thinks he is the father marries the girl, quite forgetting the past."[12]

In many parts of Italy during the sixteenth century, for instance, men sought to marry only those women who had had many amours.

[11] Briffault's "The Mothers."
[12] *Ibid.*

The exclusive possessiveness which has been encircled about the sexual relation it is patent, is only of recent evolution. The habit of lending one's wife, or even daughter, was common in many parts of Europe not many generations ago. It continued even in the fifteenth century in Holland:

"It is the custom in the Netherlands that whosoever hath a dear guest, unto him he giveth his wife in good faith." [18]

Stendahl tells of the instance of the chief magistrate whose daughter wished to keep the company of his guest for the night. When the matter was addressed to him by his wife, his reply was characteristically generous:

"With pleasure, to such a guest I will even lend my wife."

As late as the seventeenth century this custom persisted in Ireland. It still remains among the Esqimaux.

If many think that Companionate Marriage is new they should refresh their acquaintanceship with historical record. The practice of "bundling," for instance, was very akin to this modern adjustment called Companionate Marriage. All through Switzerland, for example, "bundling" was a customary practice. This form of sexual hospitality was common also among the

[18] Bebel, "Woman and Socialism."

Dutch farmers in Pennsylvania. In Scotland it had an even more marked and definite development. There the custom of "handfasting" existed as late as the sixteenth century. This custom permitted the young man to select a companion for a year, at the end of which time the couple could marry or separate, according to their own desire.[14] The idea that marriage has always been an affair of life-long duration is likewise absurd. Among many primitive peoples marriage usually lasted until the birth of a child or at best for a few years afterwards. Among the Manes of Sahara the women consider it proper to marry frequently; a long married life is condemned as unrefined and vulgar. The Abyssinians have limited or trial marriages as a general practice. The North American Indians also had trial marriages. For instance the Wyandottes had trial marriages which continued for only several days. In Persia still a woman may marry for periods varying from one hour to ninety-nine years.[15] Among the Hurons, Rev. D. Jones states that women are purchased (for marriage) by the night, week, month, or winter. The Cherokee Iroquois change wives several times a year. The Esquimaux are known for seldom keeping their wives more than a few years. In Malaya indi-

[14] Forel, "The Sexual Question."
[15] *Ibid.*

viduals marry forty and fifty times during a life-span. These variations could be multiplied without number were we to touch the habits and customs of all the different peoples in our world.

In very modern times the practice of polygamy, which ordinarily is associated with primitive and barbarous peoples—although the Biblical Jews practiced it on the basis of moral principle—was recommended by a poet no less conspicuous than John Milton and a moralist no less ingenious than John Lyser. Milton, who was a Puritan, made a plea for polygamy that was grounded in Biblical testimony:

"Either polygamy is a true marriage, or all children born in that state are spurious, which would include the whole race of Jacob, the twelve tribes chosen by God. . . . Not a trace appears of the interdiction of polygamy throughout the whole law, not even in any of the prophets."

John Becold and Jans Wilhelms, spiritual fuglemen of a sixteenth century religious sect, had wives so numerous that they multiplied into the teens—and their justification for their conduct was infused with godliness. Martin Madan, a doctor of theology, in his book, "Thelyphthora," substantiated Lyser's thesis[16] by proving with full authority that, according to the Mosaic

[16] Cf. John Lyser, "Polygamia Thriumphatrix," London, 1682, under name of Alethaeus.

code, polygamy could not be prohibited by the Christian. Another author, Sir Arthur Steven Brookes, in his "Sketches of Spain in Morocco," made another stirring defense of polygamy. In Mrs. Manley's, "Atalantis," the character Hernando defends polygamous marriage. In 1650 shortly following the peace of Westphalia, the Frankish Kreistag at Neuremburg, confronted by the decimated population which had resulted from the Thirty Years' War, passed a ruling permitting every man to marry two women.[17]

In other words, it was only a little over 275 years ago when an actual decree in favor of polygamy was issued by a Christian state in what is now Germany. And today we find Norman Haire prophesying polygamy as a possible solution for the sex problem:

"Legalized polygamy would offer many advantages . . . there are many men, and some women, who apparently need more than one person of the opposite sex to make life reasonably happy for them. Before marriage the man and women would state whether they desired the union to be monogamous or polygamous."[18]

In the matter of illegitimacy, also, attitudes have veered in different ages and under different conditions. As we have observed, in parts of Holland and in other

[17] Westermarck, "History of Human Marriage."
[18] "Hymen"-Norman Haire, Today and Tomorrow Series.

countries of Europe, a woman finds an illegitimate child no bar to marriage. Among many primitive peoples, the possession of such a child, as we now know, increased the attraction of a woman and augmented her economic value. In the heroic sagas, bastardy was a virtue; it was apostrophized rather than scorned. All the famous heroes of ancient record were bastards. King Conchobar, Cuchnalainn, Mongan, Fionn, Conairre, illustrious protoganists in Irish myth, were all bastards. To be a hero in myth bastardy seemed imperative. King Arthur and Gawain, for instance, were bastards, and in their bastardy a certain beauty was born. Many well known figures were men of illegitimate birth—Clothivig, Charles Martel, Charlemagne, Theodoric. These men made no endeavor to obscure their origin. While Alexander Hamilton lamented the fact that he was the bastard son of a Scotsman, Erasmus viewed his bastardy with approval. The honor that attached itself to bastardy finds a curious reminiscent echo in the phrase, still employed in fiction, which describes the bastard baby as a "love child." It is only with modern times that bastardy loses the splendid halo in which it has been always encircled. It was the Christian Church that first denounced adulterine children as "spurious." [19] It was not until the modern

[19] Anglo-Saxon Synod decision.

era, however, with the growth of property and the spread of acquisitive civilization that the bastard was actually disinherited in law and scorned by convention. Where the father or mother were illustrious, however, bastardy has often been a welcome privilege. The illegitimate descendants of Charles the Second had a merry time for many many years trying to prove his paternity as the authentic cause of their creation. It is chiefly with the middle classes where the inheritance of property is the main virtue that the bastard has been treated with the most cruelty and contempt. Today as we have seen, the attitude toward the illegitimate child, with the decay of bourgeois marriage and morality, has already begun to alter.

The attitude of the Christian Church itself has undergone a surprising change. In the early centuries of its era "married life was treated as absolutely unlawful." [20] St. Ambrose declared that "married people ought to blush at the state in which they are living," and Tertullian maintained that the disappearance of man was better than his propagation by sexual intercourse. The Christian hatred of woman strengthened her subjection. "Marriage and propagation are of Satan" was one of the famous proclamations of the

[20] G. Salmon, "A Historical Introduction to the Study of the Books of the New Testament."

priest Saturninus. Today the Church has reversed
its attitude completely. Marriage is now lawful and
priests and preachers confirm and bless it. The words
of Tertullian are repudiated. It is the multiplication
and not the extinction of humankind which is embodied in its opposition to birth control and abortion.
The recent consideration of Companionate Marriage
by certain Protestant sects may be only a slight indication of what later will prove another very great change.

It has been our purpose in this long recitation of
varying attitudes toward love and the sex-life to illustrate the relativity of standards and their impermanency in terms of social change. There is apparently
nothing inherent or irrevocable in any attitude. We
can only speak of values in reference to their immediate environment. They have no universal or un-
changing sanctity which can be defended as ideal.

Many ideas that have been entertained in the past
as demonstrated and definite are now seen to have been
founded upon nothing other than prejudice and rationalization. In the fanatical defense of chastity as
the basis of feminine virtue, and of postnuptial fidelity
as the test of womanly honor we discern nothing particularly lofty or spiritual. Upon analysis it becomes
simply a convention associated with a property con-

cept, attesting the demand made upon woman by a masculine morality. The idea that woman is innately, or psychologically, monogamous, while man is by nature polygamous is at once realized as absurd. In those societies in which woman is still dominant, as among the Uganda, or in Tahiti, women are as free in their sex relations and as polygamous in their affections as either ancient or modern man. Under a convention in the coming society which permits equal freedom for both men and women, then, women will be, it is logical to assume, no less polygamous or no more monogamous than men. The pressure of old habits, it is true, may tend to make woman retain an affection for monogamy even after she has acquired certain freedoms that no longer necessitate it. This reaction would be more in the form of a cultural lag however, than in one of basic tendency. When we recall the habits of famous women down the centuries, those who defied the conventions and set up freedom as their touchstone of virtue, we see only personalities that ridicule monogamy as a myth made by man for the subordination of woman. Whether it be George Sand, Sarah Bernhardt, Eleanore Duse, or in our own age the grace-winged Isadora Duncan, it is the same reaction that we always encounter. These women were the *freed* women of their times. What other women could not afford to hazard, in ages

[326]

that thundered terrifying disapprovals, these women dared with undaunted intelligence and challenging audacity. The George Sandists in nineteenth century Russia were no less scornful of the endless ennui of monogamous marriage. Wherever we turn for historical reference, we find woman more monogamous than man only when the social system makes such a relationship on her part imperative.

The new morality has already evinced this tendency in no slight form. The protest of youth has been feminine as well as masculine. Necking and petting parties have not been characterized by a marked monogamous behavior on the part of girls in contrast to that of men. If these parties do not necessarily always include the sexual act, it is merely the intervention of a lingering *mores* that retards their completion. In their expression, however, one can readily see habits of behavior that, with the entire release from this *mores,* will become definite and complete. The attitude now dominant in Soviet Russia, which regards sex relations as a matter entirely private and personal, with neither state nor convention as supervisors, is the attitude that is rapidly becoming accepted in practice if not in theory by the rest of the world.

From our previous consideration of changing morals, there should be nothing bewildering or strangely novel in this recent revolution in ethics. Scores of such revolutions have occurred in the past, with progress and recoil, and recoil and progress, expressing each in turn fundamental alterations in social and economic structure. With the candor in which sex is now beginning to be treated, there should again be no cause for astonishment. It is merely a return to an older attitude which was far more clean than the one which we have known.

It is only with the disappearance of classes, and the end of economic struggles and industrial imperialism, that the ultimate freedom inherent in the new society can ever be attained. Even in Soviet Russia such freedom will be entirely achieved only when the transitionary conditions have been superseded by the more solid foundations of a new civilization. The subjection of women in the past has been an inevitable corollary of class-dominancy and control. Subjection was one of its ineradicable attributes.

This change, to be certain, will not be simple or unfraught with pain. While man in the past has learned to conquer many of the material forces of nature, and at the present time is hastening into a period where he will learn to conquer the evils that have grown out of the private possession of property, he is only at the foothills in his attempt to conquer love. Love, as we now know, is a modern emotion. It has grown out of the sublimation of the sex urge which has developed only in the late centuries of our era. It is a highly artificial although exquisite and inspiring sentiment. Euripides, we recall, was attacked for dealing with the maudlin and repulsive spectacle of a woman in love. Love, as we of the modern age understand it, was disdained as vulgar by the Greeks. Monogamous love, of all loves, is most curiously recent. Love when it was so idealized by poet was seldom thought of as a part of marriage. Marriage was an economic transaction. Love was more often adulterous. Romantic love and monogamous marriage were contradictions until our modern age. Romantic love in the days of chivalry was particularly pagan and heroic. The monotony of marriage was its antonym. In the last few centuries there has been an endeavour to fuse these former contradictions by the idealisation of marital love and the destruction of the halo which had formerly surrounded adulterous affections. This fusion has never been very successful. However ideal in the abstract, the costs which it has extorted have been distressingly numerous and severe. The very nature of sex desire has vitiated it. The craving for variation which has always been conspicuous in the sexual history of man immediately revolted against such enforced restriction. Prostitution was only one way in which woman paid the penalty for this revolt. The double standard of morals was but one other. The racing rise of divorce in our own day is a contemporary evidence of the struggle against the old rigidities of this ethic. The new morality is youth's revolt against other forms of the same ethical system.

The conquest of love is still a hazy vision of the future. The sex problem, aside from the ethereal idealizations embodied in the love element in it, would not be so very difficult to solve. It is this love element which engages the problem with complexities of re-action that often defy analysis and solution. There is the possibility, indeed, that there is no solution at all. Even under the ideal conditions of a coming society, those ramifications of reaction derivative of the love impulse, may still carry with them many of the pangs and pains of unhappy adaptations and relationships. It is a fervent hope, naturally, that those infelicities will finally disappear. While in the past we have known the costs of repression, it is the future which will introduce to us the costs of freedom. If freedom as a theory is perfect, and as an aspiration is ideal, it is foolish of us, however, to imagine that in practice it will be accompanied by a complete absence of discord. There will still be individual dilemmas, individual diffi-culties, and individual disasters, but they will not be economic and social in character, nor the consequence of moral subjecton.

In the meanwhile, however, the present direction of sex attitudes is the only one that holds forth hope as a rich incentive. The escape from the old ethics can only be viewed as an advance.

In order to progress we must hazard new seas, and chart again the surge and undertow of course and current. The old waters have proven unnavigably shallow and treacherous. Until the new ways have been tried and tested, and the rapids conquered in the crossing, movement in this direction and that will be uncertain and insecure. These are the dangers that accompany exploration. It is the goal which inspires their risk. It is the end which defies their influence and omen.

INDEX

A

Abortion, among married women, 181; among proletarian women, 188; among syphilitic women, 188; at Carnegie Laboratories, 188; attitude toward, 175; Christian concept toward, 176-77; desire for, 178-80; economic factors in, 191, 318; effects of illegality of, 178; fatalities of in western world, 184; in primitive times, 176; in Soviet Russia, 273-9; in Tzarist Russia, 275; induced, 182, 188, 189; laws regulating in Soviet Russia, 277; since the War, 198-9; study of 31 cases of, 180-1

Abortions and Births, table showing ratio, 186

Abyssinia, 314, 320

Addison, 41

Adler, 154

Adultery, 112, 113

Africa, 314

Alimony, in Moscow, 257

American Asso. of Genito-urinary Surgeons, 135

American Birth Control League, 239, 272

American Gynecological Society, 137

American Psychopathological Association, 135

Amherst, Questionnaire distributed at, 110-13, 171

Aristotle, 176, 310

Art of Being Ruled, 49

Augustine, 65

Australia, contraceptives among savages of, 126, 314

Austria, birth rate of, 140; criminal abortions in, 185

Automobile, 93

B

Balestrini, 177

Bakeless, 50, 51

Baltimore, illegitimacy in, 194; sale of contraceptives in, 129-31, 141

Barbusse, 84

Barker, Lewellys, 142

Barnes, 50, 51, 54

Barr, Rev. J., 140

Bastardy, 322-4

Bavaria, 318

Bax, Belfort, 292

Bebel, 291

Becold, John, 321

Beddoes, Thomas, 57

Bernhardt, Sarah, 326

Birth Control, advance in methods, 142; attitude toward in Soviet Russia, 270-74; clinics in England, 268; clinics in Germany, 268; clinics in Holland, 268; clinic at Johns Hopkins

University, 142; clinics in Scandinavia, 268; knowledge of, 125; in England, 268-9; instruction in Soviet Russia, 268

Blok, Alexander, 266

Bobbed Hair, in Russia, 231

Bogdanov, 284

Boston, illegitimate fathers in, 194; illegitimacy in, 194; unmarried mothers in, 194, 199

Bovil, Col. Margaret, 192

Boys, intercourse of, 116

Braun, Lily, 204

Brazil, 52

Brieux, 84

Briffault, 317

Brooks, A. S., 322

Brown, Rev., 88

Browning, 57

Bukharin, 54

Bulinger, 66

Bumm, 185

Bundling, in Pennsylvania, 320; in Scotland, 320; in Switzerland, 319

Bunglere, 278

Butler, 57

C

Cabot, Hugh, 135

Calhoun, A. W., 295

Callinicus, 53

Calvin, 70

Carlyle, 58, 59

Carnegie Laboratories, 188

Carpenter, Edward, 249, 293

Carter, John, 52

Casanova, 127

Catherine the Great, 232

Cato, 296

Charlemagne, 323

Charles II, 127, 324

Chase, Stuart, 54

Chastity, 43; not essential, 114; contempt for, 119

Chicago, illegitimacy in, 195

Children, illegitimate, 121

China, 52, 316-7

Christianity, 59, 65; attitude toward women, 234; phallic worship in, 310

Chronicle of Nestor, 228

Clothivig, 323

Cocteau, 82

College Men: morals among, 114-5; purity of, 111; relations with prostitutes, 172

College Women, length of masturbation time, 159-60; sexual experiences of, 108-9, and 158

Companionate Marriage, 145-9, 163-8, 214, 319, 325; attempt to legalize, 164-9

Condorcet, 56

Congreve, 82

Congo, 316

Constant Wife, The, 84

Contraceptives, See Chapter VI, 36; and birth control, 133; and fear of pregnancy, 143-4; cost of early ones, 127; effects on birth rates, 268-9; in China, 127; ignorance of in medical schools, 133-4; sale of in Baltimore, 129-31 and 141

Cooper, Thomas, 58

Copulation, questionnaire on, 172-5

Corfu, 52

Crimea, 57

Criminal Abortion, in New York, 275

Cromwell, 66, 70

Cuba, 314

D

Darricarrere, 177

Dartmouth College, 107 (footnote)

Davis, Katherine B., 108, 110, 117, 123, 125, 160, 189

Decay of Capitalist Civilization, 54

Decline of the West, 49

Demosthenes, 297

Demartial, 50

Denikin, 225

Denmark, 72, 223; illegitimacy in, 198

Dewey, John, 60

Dickens, Charles, 58

Dickinson, R. L., 271

Diderot, 56

Diodorus, 314

Divorce, 62, 70, 72, 122; among Romans, 62, 65; and Church, 87-8; causes of, 76-9; divorce court, 69; in Denmark, 72; in Germany, 80; in Holland, 72; in Japan, 73; in Sweden, 72, 80; in Switzerland, 80, 261; in United States, 72, 80; increase in, 72-3; libels, 75; primitive, 63; table showing increase, 73-5

Divorce in Soviet Russia, 245, 252-65; ratio in, 264

Divorce Ratio, in Soviet Russia, 264; in United States, 264

Doctor's Dilemma, The, 85

Domestic Manners of the Americans, The, 24-7

Dreiser, T., 84

Drinking: questionnaire on, 112

Duncan, Isadora, 120

Dunn, 54

Duse, Eleanore, 326

E

Egoist, 29

Egypt, 52, 315

Eliot, George, 58, 235

Ellis, Havelock, 157, 177, 249

Elnett, 228

Engels, F., 292

England, 127, 292; birth control in, 139, 268-9; birth control clinics in, 268; early attitude toward women, 235-41; economic status of wives, 238-40

England and Wales, infant mortality rates in, 198

Erasmus, 323

Erotic attitudes, 114

Esquimaux, 319, 320

Ethelred, 235-6

Eugenic Children, 204

Euphues, 40

Ewart, 50

F

Fabre-Luce, 50

Fallopius, 127

Family, 14; disintegration of, 123

Fanatics, 17, 86

Fay, 50

Fielding, 30

Figner, Vera, 230

Fiske, Bishop, 71, 165

Flappers, 12-14

Fleet Marriages, 240

Forel, 204

France, 127, 292; attitude toward illegitimacy, 201; birth rate of, 141

Frank, Waldo, 50

Freud, 154-5, 204

Free Love, 63

Fuller, 53

G

Galsworthy, 84
Genesis of World War, 51
George, W. L., 84, 293
Georgia, 52
Germany, 208, 292, 302; abortions in, 185; attitude toward illegitimacy, 203; birth-control clinics in, 139 and 268; birthrate of, 141; illegitimate children in, 203; youth movement in—see Chapter II
Gibbs, P., 51
Girls, cared for by Salvation Army Homes, 192-3
Glikin, S. M., 245, 258, 261
Grant, Stickney, 88
Graves, Mrs., 28
Greece, Phallic worship in, 309
Gregory, Alyse, 92
Gretna Green, 240
Gros, Hans, 177

H

Haire, Norman, 322
Haldane, 53
Hamilton, Alexander, 323
Hammurabi, 234, 235
Hand of Ethelbertha, The, 30
Handfasting, 320
Hardy, T., 30, 84
Hawaii, 317
Hayes, Arthur Garfield, 75
Hellier, 188
Helvetius, 56
Herodotus, 313
Hiller, K., 177
Hinkle, Beatrice, 90
Historical Materialism, 54
Hodann; 210
D'Holbach, 56

Holland, 72, 319, 322; birth control clinics in, 139 and 268
Huber, 286
Hughes, W. C., 112
Hungary, 52

I

Ibsen, 84
Icarus, 49
Ideals, 54-8
Iliynski, I. I., 263
Illegitimate children, 193
Illegitimacy, among the proletariat, 200; attitude toward, 201, 321-2; in Denmark, 198; in Italy, 198; in Norway, 198; in Sweden, 198
India, 52
Industrial Revolution, effects on prostitution, 168
Industrialism, 35
Intercourse, age at first, 115
Ireland, 315, 319; birth control clinics in, 139
Italy, 318; contraceptives in, 127; illegitimacy in, 198; venereal infection of army, 286-7
Izvestia, 281, 282

J

Jazz, 12; and the world war, 18
Jeaffreson, 238
Jellinek, C., 177
Jenke, 54
Jews, attitude toward women, 234; phallic worship among, 310
Joad, C. M., 208
Johnson, S., 43
Johns Hopkins University, birth control clinic at, 142
Jones, D., 320

Jonson, Ben, 311
Joyce, J., 84

K

Kahn, K. H., 189-90
Kalinin, M. I., 253
Kelly, Dr. H., 183
Key, Ellen, 204
Keyserling, H., 49, 50, 82
Kiselev, 282
Kissing, 93
Knight, 54
Koichak, 225
Kollontai, 247, 294, 297, 298, 299
Kudrin', 258
Kurski, 256, 257

L

Land of the Pilgrims' Pride, 124
Lashley, L. S., 135
Legitimacy, in Soviet Russia, 245
Lenin, on position of women, 234
Lewin, 186, 187
Lewis, W., 49, 50
Lilienthal, 177
Lindsey, B., 98-108, 119, 146-8, 150, 164, 192
Luther, 66, 70
Lutz, N., 212-3
Lyly, 40
Lyser, 321
Lysistrata, 311

M

Machine Age, 35
Madagascar, 317
Madan, Martin, 321
Malaya, 320

Malleson, 86
Manley, Mrs., 322
Man is War, 52
Mandeville, Bernard de, 168
Mann, Klaus, 20
Manning, Bishop, 87, 165
Maori, abortion and birth control among, 176
Marriage, 62; as an expression of modern industrial society, 150-1; chastity unessential to, 114; civil, 66; decay of, 119; decay of as a social system, 61; monogamous, 61; sexual significance of, 122
Marriage and Divorce Laws in Soviet Russia, 252-65
Marriage Laws under the Tzar, 254
Martel, C., 323
Martineau, H., 31
Masturbation, 116, 155; among boys, 160; among college men, 157; among college women, 157-8; among girls, 160-3; among unmarried women, 162-3; among women, 156-7; in India, 155; in modern civilization, 156; questionnaire on, 112
Maugham, S., 84
Mayo, K., 155
Memel, 52
Mencken, 70
Meredith, 29
Michigan, attitude toward illegitimacy, 201
Michigan Board of Health, 187, 189
Middle Ages, 298
Mika, 126
Mill, J. S., 31
Milton, 62, 66, 69, 321

Minnesota, maternity homes in, 202

Moirova, 255-6, 259, 289

Monteglas, 50

Morality, bourgeois, see Chapter III; double, 76

Morals, questionnaire on, 111

Morand, 84

Morellet, 56

Morocco, 52

Mortality, of illegitimate infants, 197

Moscow, alimony in, 257

Mother India, 155

Mothers' Clinic, 182

Mothers, Unmarried, ages of, 193-4; footnote, 195

Municipal Birth Control Clinic, 189

Mutterschutz Movement, 204-5

N

Nathan, George Jean, 124

Nearing, Scott, 54

Nebraska, attitude toward illegitimacy, 201

Necking, 83, 95, 115, 164, 327; questionnaire on, 111-3

Nevada, attitude toward illegitimacy, 201

New Guinea, 314

New Student, 93

New Woman, 12, 32; economic independence of, 35-7

New York American, 226

New York City, criminal abortions yearly, 186-7; criminal abortions in, 275

New Zealand, 316

Nitti, 51

North Dakota, attitude toward illegitimacy, 201, 223-4

Norway, 223, 318; illegitimacy in, 198

Now it Can be Told, 50

O

Oil, 96

Old Batchelor, 82

Origin of the Next War, 50

P

Paraguay, 317

Paris, 53

Paris, venereal infection in, 287

Paris Maternite, 189

Peck and Wells, 114, 160, 172

Pennsylvania, bundling in, 320; maternity homes in, 202

Perovskaya, 230

Persia, 320

Peru, 314

Peter the Great, 231-2

Pettigrew, 54

Petting, 115, 164, 327; questionnaire on, 111-3

Phallic Worship, among Christians, Greeks, Jews, Romans, 309-10; on English stage, 310-11

Philippines, 315

Pictorial Review, 81

Plato, 176, 228

Poland, 52

Polygamy, consecutive, 68, 71, 72, 321-2

Pomponius Mela, 314

Pregnancy, among young girls, 192; terminated by abortion, 185-6, 189; treatment of in Soviet Russia, 246

Pretzang, 84

Index

Profits, 54
Proletariat, illegitimacy among, 200
Prophylactics, 119; stations, 129
Prostitutes, among youth, 167; attitude of youth towards, 173
Prostitution, decline of, 167; effect of Industrial Revolution, 168; in London from 1777 to 1860—footnote, 169; in Soviet Russia, see Chapter XV; measures to combat in Soviet Russia, 282-4, 287-8; questionnaire on, 112-3; relation to monogamy, 168-9
Protestantism, 67
Prowe, 286
Puritans, 66
Purity, absence of among college men, 111
Pygmalion, 83

Q

Questionnaire, at Amherst, 110-13 and 171; on masturbation among married women, 158, 162; to doctors about sex education, 135-8

R

Radbrush, 177
Reconstruction in Philosophy, 60
Reformation, 66
Religion, decline of, 145, 146
Restoration, 22
Revolt of Modern Youth, 98-108
Rimette, G., 189
Roman Catholic Church, 62, 66, 69

Romans, phallic worship among 309
Rome, 22
Rosetti, 14, 30
Rostovsky, 262
Rousseau, 56, 235
Ruskin, 14, 58, 59
Russell, B., 49, 50, 96, 249
Russell, D., 204
Ryan, Rev. J. A., 140

S

Sahara, 320
St. Ambrose, 324
St. Louis, illegitimacy in, 194
Salomon, Samuel, 226
Salvation Army, 192-3
Sand, George, 326, 327
Sandford, Mrs., 27
Sandist, George, Movement, 231
Sanger, Margaret, 183
Saturday's Children, 84
Scandinavia, attitude toward illegitimacy, 201-2; birth control clinics in, 139 and 268
Schriber, A., 204
Schumann, Dr. E. A., 181
Scotland, bundling in, 320
Sedley, 83
Semashko, 284, 288
Sevigny, Madame de, 127
Sex, an obsession today, 306; Christian concept of, 152-3; attitudes toward, 152; experiences among college men, 109-13; freedom of men in, 154; impermanency of attitude toward, see epilogue; instruction in medical schools, 134; instruction in Soviet Russia, 250-1; primitive attitude towards, 309

[339]

Sex in Relation to Society, 177
Shaw, G. B., 83, 85
Sherman, J., 135
Shpak, 272, 274
Sierra Leone, 317
Sin, attitude of youth toward, 114
Sinclair, Upton, 96
Slavs, 314
Smithfield Market, 238
Smyrna, 52
South Africa, 52
South Carolina, 79
Soviet Russia, 51, 52, 72, 327-8; abortion in, 178 and 273-9; attacks upon, 226; attitude toward birth control, 270-4; birth control instruction in, 268; birth control in, 139; divorce in, 245; equality of women in, 244-5; equality of morality in, 241-2; legal abortion in 1922-4, 184; legitimacy in, 245; marriage and divorce laws, 252-65; measures to combat prostitution, 282-4, 287-8; morality in, see Chapter XII; new morality in, see Chapter XVI; new moral attitude, 207-8; prostitution in, see Chapter XV; ratio of divorce in, 264; registered marriages, 255; sex instruction in, 251-2; treatment of pregnancy in, 246
Spengler, 49, 50
Stanislavsky, 120
Steele, Richard, 42, 68
Stendhal, 319
Stetson, C., 87, 88
Stillbirths, 196
Stopes, Marie, 182
Sutherland, 140

Sweden, 72, 223; illegitimacy in, 198
Swinburne, 30, 57
Switzerland: 318; bundling in, 319; divorce in, 261
Syphilis: in the United States, footnote on page 285

T

Tahiti, 317, 326
Taine, 69
Tennyson, 57
Thackeray, 30, 58
Theodoric, 323
Thomson, J., 57
Tobison, 187
Tragedy of Waste, 54
Travel Diary of a Philosopher, 49
Trollope, 24-7
Trotsky, 54
Turkey, women in, 13
Turner, J. K., 50
Twelve, The, 266
Tzarist Russia, prostitution in, 280

U

Uganda, 315, 317, 326
Ukraine, 256
Ulpianus, 177
University Woman's Clinic, 185
Unmarried Mothers, economic status of, 199; in Boston, 199
United States: 24, 72, 275, 292; birth control clinics in, 139; criminal abortions in, 187; divorce ratio in, 264; syphilis in, footnote page 285
U. S. Dept. of Commerce, 80
U. S. Dept. of State, 226

V

Vanbrugh, 83
Venereal Infection, in Italian army, 286-7; in Paris, 287
Venice, criminal abortions in, 185
Vienna, birth rate of, 141
Virginity: various attitudes toward, 315-8
Voltaire, 127
Vorden, J., 86
Vrouwen, Alex., 86

W

Wars, 51
Watson, 88, 135
Webb, B. and S., 54
Wells, H. G., 84, 85
Werfel, 84
Whither England, 54
Wied, Gustav, 85
Wiegand, 226
Wife-purchase, 64
Wilhelms, 321
Wilson, E. B., 214-5

Woman in America, 28
Women, economic advance of, 121; economic value of in early times, 236-8; political status of in Soviet Russia, 247; practices of unmarried, 117-8; under Hammurabi, 234; under monogamy, 296-7, 293, 49-50; Victorian, 29-31
World of William Clissold, 49, 85
World War, 16-21, 34, 35, 36, 48, 89; and use of contraceptives, 128-32
Wrangel, 225
Wright, Edward, 211
Wycherly, 83

Y

Yessenin, 84
Youth, attitude toward prostitutes, 173; attitudes toward sex, 98-108; insurgent, 119; movement in Germany, see Chapter XI; sexual experiences of, 98-108

Family in America

AN ARNO PRESS / NEW YORK TIMES COLLECTION

Abbott, John S. C. **The Mother at Home:** Or, The Principles of Maternal Duty. 1834.

Abrams, Ray H., editor. **The American Family in World War II.** 1943.

Addams, Jane. **A New Conscience and an Ancient Evil.** 1912.

The Aged and the Depression: Two Reports, 1931–1937. 1972.

Alcott, William A. **The Young Husband.** 1839.

Alcott, William A. **The Young Wife.** 1837.

American Sociological Society. **The Family.** 1909.

Anderson, John E. **The Young Child in the Home.** 1936.

Baldwin, Bird T., Eva Abigail Fillmore and Lora Hadley. **Farm Children.** 1930.

Beebe, Gilbert Wheeler. **Contraception and Fertility in the Southern Appalachians.** 1942.

Birth Control and Morality in Nineteenth Century America: Two Discussions, 1859–1878. 1972.

Brandt, Lilian. **Five Hundred and Seventy-Four Deserters and Their Families.** 1905. Baldwin, William H. **Family Desertion and Non-Support Laws.** 1904.

Breckinridge, Sophonisba P. **The Family and the State:** Select Documents. 1934.

Calverton, V. F. **The Bankruptcy of Marriage.** 1928.

Carlier, Auguste. **Marriage in the United States.** 1867.

Child, [Lydia]. **The Mother's Book.** 1831.

Child Care in Rural America: Collected Pamphlets, 1917–1921. 1972.

Child Rearing Literature of Twentieth Century America, 1914–1963. 1972.

The Colonial American Family: Collected Essays, 1788–1803. 1972.

Commander, Lydia Kingsmill. **The American Idea.** 1907.

Davis, Katharine Bement. **Factors in the Sex Life of Twenty-Two Hundred Women.** 1929.

Dennis, Wayne. **The Hopi Child.** 1940.

Epstein, Abraham. **Facing Old Age.** 1922. New Introduction by Wilbur J. Cohen.

The Family and Social Service in the 1920s: Two Documents, 1921–1928. 1972.

Hagood, Margaret Jarman. **Mothers of the South.** 1939.

Hall, G. Stanley. **Senescence:** The Last Half of Life. 1922.

Hall, G. Stanley. **Youth:** Its Education, Regimen, and Hygiene. 1904.

Hathway, Marion. **The Migratory Worker and Family Life.** 1934.

Homan, Walter Joseph. **Children & Quakerism.** 1939.

Key, Ellen. **The Century of the Child.** 1909.

Kirchwey, Freda. **Our Changing Morality:** A Symposium. 1930.

Kopp, Marie E. **Birth Control in Practice.** 1934.

Lawton, George. **New Goals for Old Age.** 1943.

Lichtenberger, J. P. **Divorce:** A Social Interpretation. 1931.

Lindsey, Ben B. and Wainwright Evans. **The Companionate Marriage.** 1927. New Introduction by Charles Larsen.

Lou, Herbert H. **Juvenile Courts in the United States.** 1927.

Monroe, Day. **Chicago Families.** 1932.

Mowrer, Ernest R. **Family Disorganization.** 1927.

Reed, Ruth. **The Illegitimate Family in New York City.** 1934.

Robinson, Caroline Hadley. **Seventy Birth Control Clinics.** 1930.

Watson, John B. **Psychological Care of Infant and Child.** 1928.

White House Conference on Child Health and Protection. **The Home and the Child.** 1931.

White House Conference on Child Health and Protection. **The Adolescent in the Family.** 1934.

Young, Donald, editor. **The Modern American Family.** 1932.